MORE THAN
CHAINS AND TOIL

MORE THAN CHAINS AND TOIL

A Christian Work Ethic of Enslaved Women

Joan M. Martin

Westminster John Knox Press
Louisville, Kentucky

Scripture quotations, unless otherwise indicated, are from the New
Revised Standard Version of the Bible, copyright © 1989 by the Division of Christian Education of the National Council of the Churches
of Christ in the U.S.A., and used by permission.

Book design by Sharon Adams
Cover design by Night & Day Design
Cover illustration: Jacob Lawrence, Harriet Tubman Series No. 7,
1939-40, Casein tempera on gessoed hardboard, 17⅞″ × 12″,
Hampton University Museum, Hampton, Virginia

First edition
Published by Westminster John Knox Press
Louisville, Kentucky

This book is printed on acid-free paper that meets the American
National Standards Institute Z39.48 standard. ♾

PRINTED IN THE UNITED STATES OF AMERICA

00 01 02 03 04 05 06 07 08 09 — 10 9 8 7 6 5 4 3 2 1

Library of Congress Cataloging-in-Publication Data

Martin, Joan.
    More than chains and toil : a Christian work ethic of enslaved
        women / Joan M.
    Martin.—1st ed.
        p. cm.
    Includes bibliographical references and index.
    ISBN 0-664-25800-X (alk. paper)
        1. Women slaves—United States. 2. Work ethic—United
        States—History. I. Title.
    E443.M37 2000
    305.4'09—dc21

99-086475

Contents

Preface

Work, or the lack thereof, is one of the fundamental elements of human existence that shapes our lives, our identities within our families, our communities, and the larger society in myriad ways. It is both personal and social. Functioning as such, it contains many of the core values—religious and secular—that we hold dear and that occasion social discord and strife. We name and define a significant dimension of ourselves by what we do; therefore, making meaning of life (valuing) and sustaining ourselves and our loved ones through our livelihood is a complex human endeavor. Womanist religious ethicists and theologians often have stated that naming and understanding our identities is crucial to the honest, straightforward way in which we do our work as blackwomen of faith, and as ministers, scholars, and teachers. To do so is, in fact, part of the work. Therefore, in a work about *work* it is important to share with readers who I am in relation to my theme, and why I value writing about work.

Today, one of the ways in which I name and understand myself is as a theological ethicist—that is, by what I do in the public and religious arenas and by what I teach and have the luxury to contemplate. It wasn't always this way, but how did I get here? Growing up, my parents gave me and my siblings a legacy of work—they impressed upon me that hard, decent, and honest work, coupled with a good education and a deep faith in Jesus, were sufficient to gain respect in the world. And they tried their very best to model what they believed, particularly as African Americans in what they understood to be a racially divided and therefore unsafe society.

Both my father's and mother's life experiences bore out these truths. After a childhood as a sharecropper's son in east Texas, my father was compelled to leave the South (with its hatred of blacks) and obtain a land-grant education. Eventually, he would become a program director in a Veterans' Administration Hospital through the civil service. My mother, the daughter of an immigrant Jamaican tailor and a Rockland County, New York, domestic worker, was a public school elementary teacher. To secure her first teaching position, she risked integrating the faculty of a small, New Jersey school district. While sharecropping seemed to be a subject my father would rather leave buried in the past, my mother frequently told stories about my grandmother—a domestic and laundress—and the ways in which black domestic workers organized their church lives. My maternal grandmother had handed down stories about black folks holding their own Sunday services in the evening so that they could work during the day to serve Sunday dinner to "white families on the hill" immediately following worship services. She also told tales of her own escapades with friends as they worked for my grandfather, driving around town after school delivering tailoring to his customers. Like countless other young people of previous generations, I learned from such stories that *the church* was the place where my grandparents' occupations were honored and given dignity rather than ridiculed and exploited. In *the church,* cooks, domestics, sharecroppers, and janitors as well as teachers, doctors, and store-owners were cherished for what they did and who they were as children of the living God.

Both my parents worked outside the home every workday of each week, year in and year out, until they retired from their respective careers. Both parents also worked *inside* the home, sharing child care, nurturing, cooking, cleaning, doing home improvement projects, and providing homework assistance. The result was that my siblings and I were the inheritors of the truth, the legacy, and the material resources to start us modestly toward attaining whatever dreams and goals we could fashion for ourselves. We had both our mother and father as work and parenting role models as well as extended family members among whom were steelworkers, Pentecostal ministers, seamstresses, tractor trailer drivers, doctors, Air Force pilots, and county sheriffs, to name a few.

My mother and father—and my aunts, uncles, and older cousins—received and provided leadership training in the church, further exemplifying the close-knit relationship between faith, family, and work life. This rich family background of work encompassed values which emerged from a Baptist, Pentecostal, and a fourth-generation Black Presbyterian heritage; a familial history with roots in enslavement, sharecropping, and domestic service; and a work history including black small business ownership and wage labor in civil service and public education. This diversity was undergirded by black Christian and black cultural values of the working and middle-class strata. We were expected to prepare ourselves for more than just a job; we were expected to dream of careers. Rather than living in dependence on another's land or in another's building, we were expected to grasp the American dream of owning our own homes. We were expected to always be in a position to pay off our debts. My parents—who had lived through the Great Depression as adolescents and young adults—valued self-reliance. We were expected to become active in civic and community organizations and in the church, as well as to raise families, and to meet our obligations to tithe to church and community missions. One's work provided the means by which all these things could and should be accomplished.

Accordingly, I went to work at the age of nine—that is, I gave myself a job and became self-employed. I sold Christmas cards every fall to family, friends, neighbors, teachers, and church members so that I could have my own Christmas shopping money. My parents helped, too. Little did I know! My mother and father each year actually "financed" my endeavor out of their modest resources because I could never sell enough boxes of cards, no matter how hard I worked. Nevertheless, I was motivated, industrious, and proud of my labors. By age fifteen, with my social security card in hand, I had found a real paying job at minimum wage as a clerk in a downtown Newark, New Jersey, bookstore, working after school and on weekends. Through high school, college, and seminary, I worked at full- and part-time jobs while registered for a full course load. And even in doctoral studies, I was a worker in part-time wage and professional positions. I have been privileged to enjoy consistent work for nearly thirty years, twenty-three of which have been as a fully employed professional in the church.

On the evening of my ordination, as we sat in the worship service, my older cousin leaned forward, tapped me on the shoulder, and said, "Now look girl, you had better not mess up." She wasn't talking about forgetting to say, "I do" and "I will" to the Presbyterian constitutional questions. Nor was she saying, "Don't fall on your face when they tell you to kneel for the 'laying on of hands.'" No, what she meant was deeper than family embarrassment, and more ancient than the three generations of Black Presbyterians present that night. My cousin was reminding me of my responsibility to the African American people in a predominantly white denomination, and in white America. Throughout my entire life, then, work has been a central element—one with multiple meanings and dimensions.

Within the assumptions of these various aspects of life, a person's social location—identity and work—is bound together in a constellation of relations which connect personal and familial histories to social ones, and social histories to the operation of society's superstructures, including that of work. To understand my personal history, it is appropriate to explore the African American social experience of work, the blackwomen's[1] social experience of work, the role of the church and its theological ethics, and the societal structures which have framed the concomitant structures of history and moral agency and value. In this way this book is "personal, theological, and political." It is grounded in the relationship between religious belief and intellectual curiosity. Finally, it is set in the context of the sacred hope for freedom in and for the African American community and the secular goal of economic justice and meaningful work in the United States.

Cambridge, 1999

Acknowledgments

A very special colleague, mentor, and friend once told me that, in order to write a book, you must have a deep and abiding passion for the subject so that you can get over the "down times" that emerge from the first page to the last one. In this process I have also learned a great deal about the passion of one's colleagues, mentors, and friends that sustains a writer in the "love affair" of creating a book. Chuck Rawlings, an untiring advocate for the rights of workers over the last two-plus decades, inspired me to formulate my passion for understanding work and human meaning, beginning with my own roots in the African American religious tradition and in theological ethics. I will forever be indebted to Chuck for the clarity that he gave me that has nourished this endeavor over thirteen years. Equally important were Professors John C. Raines, Katie G. Cannon, Bettye Collier-Thomas, and Gibson Winter at Temple University, who steadfastly guided this work into its dissertation form with sharply focused criticism and the demand for excellence.

A word of appreciation goes to the fine research staffs at Temple University's Paley Library, The Schomburg Library of the New York Public Library, Widener and Lamont Libraries of Harvard University, and the curators of the Federal Writers' Project—Works Progress Administration Slave Narrative Collection of the Library of Congress. Their skill, thoughtfulness, and dedication to their mission have made the search for manuscripts a wonderful adventure.

I am very grateful for the institutional support I have received at key moments as a new scholar. My deepest thanks goes to The Episcopal Divinity School for resources from its Theological Writing Fund and the all-important release time from academic responsibilities, including sabbatical leave. Most dear to my heart has been the collegial encouragement and assistance from Academic Deans Fredrica Harris Thompsett and Joanna Dewey, and Professors Kwok Pui Lan, Angela Bauer, and Gale Yee. As white feminists, Asian, and Asian American feminists, they have joyfully shared in my search for and articulation of the voices of my African American women ancestors. Their technical assistance and willingness to read proposals and drafts, and to listen to my frustrations about my writing, have been invaluable.

Further encouragement and critique of my work has been forthcoming from the participants of the 1999–2000 Lilly Foundation/American Academy of Religion Workshop, "Mining the Motherlode: Teaching the African American Religious Experience." Facilitation team members Emilie Townes, Will Coleman, Carolyn Jones, and A. G. Miller have surrounded me with intellectual, spiritual, and scholarly nurture, and the colleague participants honed several key issues with both insight and humor. Likewise, a special word of thanks goes to independent scholar Anne Bathurst Gilson for her editorial work on the manuscript and to Beverly W. Harrison for her gracious gift of personal and professional contacts in the world of religious studies publishing.

I want to say "thank you" to the Editorial Board of Westminster John Knox Press, and a very special "thank you" to my editor, G. Nick Street. Nick has been thoughtful, patient, and saintly, and his work on the manuscript has been indispensable in making it the product that it has become.

In the course of writing this book, I owe much to these many and varied colleagues, mentors, and friends. I have taken all their constructive words to heart to make this work the best I have to offer. Their contributions are evident throughout the book. Indeed, so also are the weaknesses probably, and I alone gladly take responsibility for those. Lastly, I want to thank my family, and to let you all know that it is from you that I have learned to love work, and in part, live well by working. With ever-abiding love, thank you to my mother, Gwendolyn L. Martin; my siblings Jerry and Janet; and to Rowland Sr., whose spirit for and love of literature I will hold in my heart forever. And I give thanks to the Spirit of Love for Barbara Weaver, Alice McIntyre, and Binta Colley, the three little girls Juana, Lanie, and Emily, and the mischievous bearded collies, Sundance and B'Elanna, who all remind me that beyond work, there is play!

Introduction

At first glance, to juxtapose the reality of enslaved women's work with a notion of a work ethic, particularly one grounded in religious and community values, seems like a contradiction and a futile exercise in testing an illogical hypothesis. On the one hand, the work done by enslaved women in the antebellum was coercive, exploitative, and dehumanizing as part of the system and structure of chattel slavery in the United States. On the other hand, the notion of a work ethic in the U.S. religious, economic, educational, and cultural ethos has been portrayed as tantamount to a recipe for the successful and *virtuous* life. Placed together, both elements appear to be like oil and water—they just don't mix. In the early stages of this book, the research seemed to indicate just this fact.

More Than Chains and Toil is a book that focuses on the deeper dimensions of the facts: the lives of enslaved blackwomen as moral agents and their struggle to create positive meaning out of the very element which defined their lives—work. In the antebellum, the labor of blackwomen, blackmen, and blackchildren was not only owned by someone else, but also more important, the vast majority of African Americans did not own themselves. Literally, others owned them; they were chattel. This fundamental fact makes chattel unique among the labor systems in U.S. history. In this book, I explore the connection between how work provides human meaning (value) in situations when the content and the context of work are dehumanizing for a particular group, and they are stigmatized by the social constructions of race, gender, and economics, held in place by Christian theology and ethics. Thus, work is the historical, social, theological, and ethical ("theo-ethical") departure point for understanding work and human meaning for African American Christian ethics in contemporary society.

My choice of the word *discover* is intentional. From my own familial history situated in the historical past of U.S. and Caribbean enslavement, I wanted to know how I had come to hold a strong "work ethic." Moreover, I sought to understand the relationship between my work ethic, my middle-class background as an African American woman at the dawn of the new millennium, and the contemporary and possible future employment situation in the U.S. for blackpeople. My colleague Kwok Pui Lan found in her work on colonialism and Christianity in China that the word *discover* is "used to signify the move from an external perspective toward a more internal approach, one that sees the history of a given non-western society in its own terms and from its own point of view rather than as an extension of western history."[1] While chattel slavery is the context of the work ethic I explore, the non-Western, African origins of blackpeople in the U.S. arose from British and European colonialism and the ensuing attempts to suppress the African cultures of those it enslaved. My task has been both literal and figurative—finding blackwomen's historical experience of work, finding *internal perspectives* of blackwomen themselves, and finding their *external perspectives* on colonialism, enslavement, and oppression. Blackwomen have embarked upon such discoveries before in our "herstories" and spiritual/intellectual work as evidenced by the work of Anna Julia Cooper and Ida B. Wells.[2]

The rich history and tradition of African American (Protestant) Christianity, specifically its community ethos that has valued human dignity in the face of white racism, have also shaped this journey of discovery. No matter what negative images, stereotypes, and experiences the larger predominantly white society has tried to instill in African Americans, the black church has countered that teaching and experience, affirming that blackpeople are the subject of God's love and justice. Furthermore, I have come to understand and incorporate into this journey the reality that human dignity is affected not only by race, but also by sexual, gender, and class systems of oppression. Gender has been a distinct, yet interrelated, form of oppression affecting blackwomen's lives in the black church and the black community as well as in the larger society. This "colonization of the female mind and culture"[3] within the African American community and the larger, dominant society gives me pause in researching and writing about blackwomen's lives. This work is not meant to be a romanticization of blackwomen's realities. Each of these realities has increasingly influenced my perspectives and understanding of ethics regarding human dignity, work, education, family, social relations, and religion. In light of the intersecting and multilayered nature of race, sex/gender, and class oppression, I have found resonance in the terms "womanist" and "feminist" as self-identifying and positive names to embrace a way of ethically living in, acting in, and analyzing the contemporary situation of society.

Throughout the course of this book, the notion of a womanist/ feminist faith, self-in-community, and critical analytic perspective will unfold. As it does, this particular "women's way of knowing," believing, seeing, doing, and reflecting will suggest that the web of life for African American women is a complex, diverse, and multilayered cloth in which the fullness of our humanity is woven and understood. In reality, to know, to believe, to see, to do, and to reflect as a blackwoman *is to be* human—an affirmation in the face of a constant barrage from society of "otherness." In other words, our humanity is found in the intersection of our past experience, our present struggle, and our hope for and vision of the future. This humanity is revealed in the ongoing reflection on and action for our struggle—the struggle for freedom of our ancestors, for quality of life with all *who are* and all *that is,* and our historic liberation project which is eschatological in scope. A womanist/feminist perspective is thus a conscious and self-conscious element in *living* humanly. And as the lives of a

segment of enslaved blackwomen demonstrate, the womanist/
feminist lens is constructively critical of blackwomen's Christian
faith and witness, while continuing to empower and give meaning
to blackwomen's experience of faith and life in the church and
world. Within the context of this study, work and human meaning
is investigated from this standpoint.

Menial toil was the reality of blackwomen's work and the
purpose for their existence, beginning with indentured service in
the 1620s and later codified in colonial regulations, states' laws,
and social practices of chattel slavery from the 1650s until 1865.
They worked as field hands for planters' tobacco crops in Con-
necticut and Virginia. In New Jersey, Pennsylvania, and New
York State, they were dairymaids and brewers of beer for the
farmers who owned them. They were cooks, mammies for
planters' children, and servants for planters' wives in North and
South Carolina. In Georgia and Alabama, they were nursemaids
for the planters' deathbeds and breeders for the planters' labor
supply. They were cotton pickers and seamstresses in Mississippi
and Texas, and in Louisiana they were concubines. For blackwomen, enslavement meant restriction to two basic types of
work—domestic service and traditional women's work in the
home as a workplace for sewing, canning, and midwifery, and
manual labor in fields planting, cultivating, and harvesting; erect-
ing and mending fences; and even building roads. The latter was
so physically taxing as to be considered men's work. As chattel,
they were the property of others so they never received paid com-
pensation or remuneration for their labor. African American
enslaved women were exploited in their work on three counts: as
racially black, sexually women, and degraded workers. Thus,
their work was "menial."

Within enslaved communities, blackwomen's labor was profoundly important. They nourished, sustained, and enlivened the
common purpose of survival, family life, and culture. Work as
wives and mothers maintained family against many odds. These
very efforts forged the foundations of community welfare, as
blackwomen simultaneously understood that the interests of their
families, extended and fictive kinfolk, and community were bound

to the interests of blackpeople as an oppressed people. Enslaved blackwomen often fed family, other community members, and strangers from the leftovers of the slaveholder's table or with the rations from her own cabin cooking pot. As mothers, wet nurses, and root workers, enslaved women often met the medical and spiritual needs of the slave quarter's children, menfolk, and pregnant women, healing and curing injured bodies and broken spirits. On occasion, the African American woman became the protector of and even spokesperson for the welfare of the slave quarter in relation to the slaveowner. And they suffered in and through their work as well—physically, mentally, emotionally, and spiritually. This, too, was blackwomen's work reality.

Countless volumes have been written in the last three decades on the African American experience of enslavement, and increasingly on the black social history of work in the United States. This development, in turn, has fostered theological and ethical reflection by the African American community of religious scholars and their critique of normative religious ethics regarding this experience. However, black religious scholars have only superficially explored the theme of work, and a most enigmatic silence has persisted in religious ethics given that work was a central feature of life of enslaved women and men. Hence, this book is a beginning exploration of the religious moral agency of enslaved women through work and its meaning in their struggle for survival and quest for freedom.

More Than Chains relates the experiential realities in the lives of enslaved women and their social world in the antebellum concerning the relationship between moral agency, work, and human meaning. Drawing on slave narratives and related sources, the book uncovers and discusses four distinct characteristics of an enslaved women's work ethic. Fundamentally, I argue that the work ethic of enslaved Christian women was different from both the Protestant tradition's understanding of work from the Reformation notion of vocation, calling, and work, and the work ethic of antebellum slaveholders. I employ a womanist/black feminist racial and gender analysis—integral to my argument—combined with poststructural and political science theory.

Chapter 1 focuses on the lives of enslaved women as encompassed in the social world of enslavement—a world that is racialized and gendered—and only recently examined from the
perspective of African American women historians and religious
scholars. The nature of that social world, including its theological
dimensions, is best examined through the utilization of women's
slave narratives. Viewing slave narratives from the perspective of
"sacred text" provides a lens that assists in seeing the moral
agency of enslaved women in the social world of work.

In preparation for a detailed examination of women's slave narratives, chapter 2 develops a multi-methodological background
for reading the narratives. The everyday experience of enslaved
women lives entails the intersection of religion, race, and gender
within the institution of slavery. Therefore, three primary methods
are employed for the hermeneutical task of discovering a work
ethic embedded in the everyday lives of enslaved women. In particular, a womanist method reveals blackwomen's visibility in the
institution. A "logic of practice" renders deeply structured practices more visible within lived experience and written texts. A
political theory of "hidden scripts" helps in explicating moral
agency. Lastly, a fourth perspective is assumed—the legacy of
African traditional religious morals—to challenge the notion that
the enslaved derived moral values from solely western Christian
sources.

Together, chapters 3 and 4 form the heart of the book's argument. From a close reading of the women's slave narratives,
1830–1865, four characteristics of enslaved Christian women's
work ethics are identified and discussed. These characteristics
arise from using the methods of chapter 2 in order to view how
enslaved women acted as moral agents in their day-to-day work
world of enslavement. The characteristics also are examined in
light of the structure of slavery itself and the racialized and gendered nature of moral action and theological reflection of enslaved
women. Moving from the critical analysis of enslaved women's
work ethic characteristics, chapter 4 discusses this work ethic in
relation to the Christian tradition biblically, theologically, and
culturally.

I conclude *More Than Chains* by pondering whether the future will be the same as the past in light of enslaved women's experience of work and human meaning. While I can neither know the future nor predict the social and theological history of work coming toward us, I do believe the work ethic of enslaved women gives us clues to use to discern the moral path ahead through challenges and insights to the notion of a work ethic.

1

Unearthing and Remembering: Emancipating the Lives of Enslaved Women

I tell here a circumstance that happened after I had grown much older and stronger [as a child]. I had been in the field a good ways from the house, helping him [Master Kibbler] to haul logs. Our work was done, . . . when a drove of hogs ran in to get the clover that was growing in a part of the field. He called to me to drive out the hogs. I clapped my hands together, shouted, "Shoo! shoo!" This frightened the horses, and Kibbler was unable to control them; and rushing through the gateway, the team hit the side post, tearing it up from its place. Of course, all this made him very angry; and, of course, I was to blame for it all. As soon as he could hold the horses, he turned and shouted to me to drive out the hogs, set the post in the ground, and get back to the house by the time he did, or he would whip me so I would remember it . . .

I have sometimes tried to picture what my life might have been could I have been set free at that age; and I have imagined myself with a young girl's ambition, working hard and carefully saving my earnings, then getting a little home with a garden where I could plant the kind of things I had known in the South, then bringing my sisters and brothers to share with me these blessings of freedom.[1]

Bethany Veney, known also as "Aunt Betty," in 1889 wrote a "little book containing the simple story of one of the five millions

9

of human beings who, less than thirty years ago, were bought and sold like beasts of burden, in fifteen out of thirty-two States." At that time, she recalled the events that had occurred in her life as an enslaved child and woman. Veney also reflected on her sense that slavery was a fact in our national history that was largely overlooked and to the "generation now coming upon the stage of action" was almost unknown.[2]

Three remarkable elements emerge from the words of Aunt Betty. First, work in enslavement was from childhood through one's entire lifetime. Bethany Veney was a young girl, perhaps in early adolescence, when she was expected to assist in hauling logs, to know how to drive hogs, lift and reset fence posts in the ground, and to obediently come to her master for a whipping if her work did not please him. Moreover, the work described in this passage illustrates that in the lives of many ordinary enslaved women the gendered division of labor did not so strictly apply as in the dominant cultural mythology of femininity and masculinity. Enslaved women and men often were given the same work regimens, especially on small plantation holdings. Furthermore, work and obedience were normal expectations in enslaved life and were undergirded by emotional abuse and the threat of physical violence. As illustrated, Veney tells of running away, suffering intense hunger, and experiencing the cold and rain for almost three days due to her fear of being whipped by her master for this incident.

Second, freedom was a vital and constant feature of the enslaved imagination even though its actual prospects might have seemed remote or nonexistent. Writing her narrative after years of enslavement and later emancipation, Veney still vividly recalled the childhood dreams of freedom and the life she might have lived had it not been for slavery. Freedom meant possibly reaping the rewards of "ambition, hard work and carefully saved earnings, then getting a little home and garden," along with enjoying the companionship of siblings. Clearly, Veney understood that freedom entailed several essential elements: goals, effort, and diligent work; the opportunity to make good on the modest "blessings" of a home and garden by the sweat of one's labor; and the right to claim the bonds of family without the fear of sale. For her, this understanding stood in stark contrast to stereotypical images of "the slave" that included laziness, docility toward and acceptance of enslavement, and childish dependency.

Third, Aunt Betty understood that by writing her own story, she was writing *into* history the story of millions of women, men, and children whose multigenerational struggle was slipping from the nation's memory as if it had never occurred. Narratives of the antebellum and postbellum periods such as Veney's recorded and told the history of slavery not from the point of view of the lawmakers and their debates, nor the slaveholders and proslavery apologists, nor U.S. and Confederate presidents or military generals. Rather, the narratives recount a history of those who actually experienced enslavement, those who were not permitted by law in many places to learn to read or write, and those who were never supposed to write themselves into human existence, much less human dignity.

The Slave Narrative as a Source of Emancipatory History

Enslaved women's narratives *set free* the lives of women who were propertied objects and artifacts of others' history; the narratives made them the subjects of history. They provide a source of enslaved witnessing which can be characterized both as an individual document and as a wide-ranging, broad corpus of autobiographical and narrative writing that includes journals, newspaper articles, magazine interviews, church records, personal letters, and amanuensic autobiographies of ex-enslaved women and men. Narratives reveal the institution of slavery as experienced by enslaved people in their struggle for freedom in the antebellum United States.[3]

In 1703, the first slave narrative was published in Boston and was titled *Adam,* "servant of John Saffin, Esquire."[4] It began a long process of enslaved testimony that culminated with the appearance of the narrative of George Washington Carver in 1944. During this 241-year period, the slave narratives took on a variety of specific purposes. For many of those written or dictated from

1703 to 1830, the narrators sought to expose the social prejudice which they endured, a prejudice that was not limited to their economic status as slaves but was fundamentally based on skin color and the wider conditions of servitude. Often this testimony was written in the style of a nineteenth-century American adventure narrative in which the enslaved person's intelligence, industriousness, talents, and cunning were set forth to show the normative human personality of the enslaved in contrast to the picture portrayed by slaveholders.

A second historical period, from 1830 to 1865, saw a different purpose emerge in the slaves' use of narrative, namely that of propaganda and political entreaty in the abolitionist movements, both black and white. The enslaved author, in flight to the North, now utilized her or his narrative to attack the *institution* of chattel slavery as the root problem. In this dramatic shift, enslaved narrators provided evidence from their own lives, and those within their enslaved community whom they knew, to indict the "peculiar institution" as evil and inhuman.

Several factors gave rise to this change in the purpose of the slave witness to chattel existence. Agriculture, geography, and political circumstances were crucial factors. Expansion from the Old South into the West and Southwest was being fueled by soil depletion, changing market conditions, and technological advances in crop harvesting. Politically and juridically, this westward expansion raised the issue of the balance between free versus slaveholding states, representing issues of power, economic interests, and long-treasured social patterns.[5] A further challenge confronted both proslavery and abolitionist causes in the U.S. with the abolition of slavery in the British Empire. Moreover, fugitive slave reports, and new and more restricted laws in slaveholding states, indicated an increase in cruelty, where even torture was used against the enslaved. Slave revolts and insurrections, such as that led by the Rev. Nat Turner, brought a frightened and punitive response from the slavocracy. In their own fashion and language, the voices of fugitives and the ex-enslaved testified to these new developments and resulted in slavery itself coming under systematic judgment.

During this period (and later in the 1920s and '30s), a vital form of slave narrative was the interview. While many narrators were literate, others created their narratives through a question-and-answer format in which the ex-enslaved presented their remembrances of slavery. Sometimes these narratives were verbatim interviews. In other cases, they were created through the process of amanuensis. This left many narratives reshaped by the motives of the scribe or editor, especially if such persons were active in the white abolitionist movement. An example of a woman's narrative is that of *Louisa Picquet, the Octoroon: A Tale of Southern Slave Life*. The interviewer, a Rev. Hiram Mattison, was interested in the moral depravity of slavery and utilized Picquet's life as a concubine to level a moralistic antislavery potboiler that displayed remarkable insensitivity to Picquet's personal suffering or her public persona as a blackwoman. Still others, decidedly the interviews of the American Freedman's Inquiry Commission (AFIC) under Lincoln's Departments of War and State, demonstrate that slave-narrative interviews were solicited for the purpose of determining public policy and humanitarian aid when, after the war, all slaves would be freed.

Within the diverse motivations for slave narratives in this period, the outstanding feature is the same. While the slave personality remains center stage, it does so only in order to advance an understanding of the collective victimization of African Americans as chattel. Furthermore, they critique the institution of slavery and slaveholders as the radical, root problem rather than that of the so-called "nature" of enslaved people.

The last period of slave narrative extends from the post-Civil War and Reconstruction period to 1944. The narratives of this era are presented as reminiscences of slavery to remind the reader of the struggle of African American women and men for emancipation and the continuing need for justice. The narrative of Bethany Veney is one such example. *A Slave Girl's Story—Being an Autobiography of Kate Drumgoold* is another. In her introduction, Drumgoold, again writing blackpeople into history, states, "This sketch is written for the good of those that have written and prayed that the slaves might be a freed people, and have schools and books and learn to read and write for themselves . . ."[6] She then demonstrates a further goal of the postbellum narrative— exhorting her readers in the cause of racial uplift. Drumgoold boldly writes:

> We as the Negro Race, are a free people, and God be praised for it. We as the Negro Race, need to feel proud of the race, and I for one do with all my heart and soul and mind, knowing as I do, for I have labored for the good of the race, that their children might be the bright and shining lights. And we can see the progress we are making . . .[7]

Other narrators, particularly women, often hold up the memory of the slave mother (which, in many instances were their own mothers) and condemn the hypocritical standards of purity, delicateness, and refinement by which the African American woman was judged. In her postbellum narrative, Lucy Delaney recalls, "Dear, dear mother! how solemnly I invoke your spirit as I review these trying scenes of my girlhood, so long agone! Your patient face and neatly-dressed figure stands ever in the foreground of the checkered time; a figure showing naught to an onlooker but the common place virtues of an honest woman!"[8] Still other narratives provide the opportunity to espouse strategies by which blacks could live within the confines of Jim Crowism following Reconstruction and accommodate to the reality of race relations of the late nineteenth and early twentieth centuries.

Fisk University, in the years 1927–1929, the University of Chicago in collaboration with Fisk, in 1929; and Southern University created privately funded sociological and anthropological projects to interview ex-slaves and, in some cases, ex-slaveowners. A similar type of project followed at Prairie View State College during the years 1935–1938, resulting in more than 400 interviews. These interviews, conducted by black graduate students and research staff, recorded information free of white racial bias which tainted the results of the Federal Writers' Project—Works Progress Administration Slave Narrative Collection (1933 to 1938).

These series of interviews in the 1920s and '30s recorded the recollections of the last remaining ex-enslaved men and women, people who were no more than five to ten years old when slavery ended. The WPA Slave Narrative Collection—uneven in content, uneven in interviewing method, uneven in national and state and local implementation, and plagued by the racism of the predominantly white interviewers—nevertheless remains the largest composite of slave narratives in the voice of the masses of ordinary, everyday slaves. Although the purpose of the WPA Slave Narrative Collection was anthropological, capturing an aspect of American folklore rapidly becoming extinct, it has provided rich historical insight into the everyday practices of slavery and its social relations. They are different from, and in many cases in opposition to, the view of slavery put forth by slaveholder and proslavery sources.

In these and in other ways, the slave narratives provide a "continuous record of that institution"[9] which reveal a legacy of the struggle for self-expression by humans considered to be nonhumans. These pages expound the thought, language, and action of those yearning for political, social, religious, and economic rights required for human dignity—those at the time the country termed "chattel." In the face of proslavery apologetics and its normative social history, the resilience of the slave narrative as historical documentation unveils the perversity of American life caught in the continuing perniciousness of its white racism.

Blackwomen's Slave Historiography and Narratives

When Marion Starling completed her doctoral dissertation in 1946, she decided to forgo publishing it out of deference to her family—her grandfather had been enslaved.[10] Following in the footsteps of African American scholars like Carter G. Woodson and W. E. B. Du Bois, each having made reference to or utilized only a small number of narratives, Starling had utilized enslaved and free black sources—autobiographies, journals, newspapers, and ex-slave interviews—to provide documentation on a variety of perspectives regarding the nature of enslavement and the postenslavement condition of blacks. However, at that time, slave historiography was a field dominated by white male scholars. Originating with Ulrich B. Phillips' *American Negro Slavery* in 1918, such scholars remained disinterested in the use of African American sources as documentation for slave history and any new interpretations that might result. "So great were the historians' suspicions of inauthenticity that for many years American historians had ignored the narratives because they were convinced that these tales were the creations of Abolitionists."[11]

In response, African American and progressive white scholars began to challenge the prevailing historical view of slavery and the character and nature of enslaved persons. In the 1930s and '40s historians focused on "slave resistance," in the 1950s on the nature of the "slave" in the "peculiar institution," and by the late 1960s on studies of slaves and slave culture.[12] Interpretations of enslavement, particularly by African American scholars, critiqued the social history of slavery using theoretical and methodological frameworks from anthropology, economics, and psychology as well as from black historical sources. In doing so, they began to challenge notions of slavery by critiquing kinship patterns, the capitalist mode of production and social relations, and western psychological models.

For example, George Rawick considers the context of the enslaved culture-creation as one of a slave economy within a capitalistic world framework. African patterns of work survived, according to Rawick, but could no longer be seen as cooperative and/or kinship-based economies and work patterns as they had been in West and Central Africa. In the production of the slave economy based on market export within America's emerging capitalism, the West and Central African work patterns and value changed.[13] No longer was work understood in relation to the kin-group but rather as an ethic of subversion: destruction of implements, clandestine theft of food, and "hideaway" time off, as well as the working of provision grounds to supplement the community's and family's diet, or to sell for cash.[14]

However, most of the black and white male historians at the time did not differentiate between the experience of men and that of women in enslavement.[15] There was no self-critique on the basis of gender, so neither theoretical nor methodological frameworks uncovered the "blackwomen's" experience of enslavement. At best, the traditional and "token" blackwomen figures—mammies and concubines—were given mention, and at that, only from within the constructs of black male perspectives on slavery and manhood or masculinity (although such perspectives were never openly identified as such by black male scholars). Generally, only Sojourner Truth and Harriet Tubman, the "exceptional" blackwomen, were recognized in the prevailing scholarship.

In 1985, two major works heralded the growing literary and historical attention being given to the experience of blackwomen in the United States, including enslaved women in the colonial and antebellum periods. Deborah Gray White's *Ar'nt I a Woman? Female Slaves in the Plantation South* and Jacqueline Jones' *Labor of Love, Labor of Sorrow: Black Women, Work and the Family from Slavery to the Present*[16] substantively addressed the history, culture, resistance, and struggle for quality of life of enslaved women. Using a variety of sources—in particular, enslaved women's narratives and memoirs, and the Works Progress Administration (WPA) and Federal Writers Project (FWP) Slave Narrative Collections—these historians created new perspectives and interpretations regarding the role of enslaved women in U.S. history and in understandings of enslaved culture. In addition to utilizing enslaved and ex-enslaved women's sources, blackwomen historians and literary critics developed black-oriented gender analysis of black and white male sexism, patriarchy, and white female racism.

Within the surviving slave narratives, twelve percent were written or dictated by blackwomen. Within their testimonies, these narratives depict the many similarities that the general lifelong condition of enslavement held for blackwomen and men. Yet, they illustrate slavery's sharp and marked differences as well, making the enslaved blackwoman's experience a very particular and distinguishable experience from that of her male counterpart.

White makes a salient critique of black male historians' work in the 1970s, especially in their reappropriation of enslaved manhood and masculinity, often at the expense of blackwomen.[17]

She calls attention directly to the refutation of the "sambo" slave personality from the male point of view—which does not discount the female stereotype infused in that white racist image. Furthermore, male writings about the role of enslaved women lack focus on the maintenance and centrality of the enslaved family, and on the woman's role in the slave community leadership in general. Enslaved women's sexuality is discussed from a male-gendered gaze, particularly in examples of the sexual division of labor in the slave work regime. While understanding this development in light of white historical traditions and the political context of the rise of black slave historiography, blackwomen historians' voices have arisen as a necessary and important corrective to the perspectives on the enslaved community and culture.

Race, gender, and class analysis are necessary both to making enslaved women's experiences visible and to interpreting those experiences. Reading and utilizing enslaved women's narratives viewed from interrelated race, gender, and class analysis permits the investigation of several key elements in the lives of enslaved women:

1. the distinct nature of enslaved women's work life and regimen in relation to the institution of slavery and to the slave quarter community life—family and social;

2. the nature of enslaved women's forms of resistance, sabotage, and insurrection for self and community against slavery (without arguing for a predominant form of any of these three activities or categories);

3. the African culturally oriented sensibilities used in enslaved women's transformation and creation of slave culture;

4. the high degree of gender consciousness and racial solidarity which enslaved black women developed; and

5. the fullness of work creativity in the midst of toilsome labor, and the dreams that African American enslaved women had for themselves and their children, which are reflected in African American

enslaved culture, both in its strength and in its weakness.

All of these elements in the narratives provide a more comprehensive view of the enslaved female, as well as the social relations among blackwomen, their men, and their children.

Regarding the emphasis on enslaved blackwomen's work, Jones makes a critical comment that combines the nature of work, the definition of work, and its meaning to enslaved women. She maintains that, if the definition of work is one of any activity that leads directly or indirectly to the production of market goods, then everything enslaved blackwomen did was work. Even their efforts to care for themselves and their families helped to maintain the owner's work force and to enhance its overall production.[18]

Within this sentiment is revealed the nature of female plantation enslavement. There was one system for men and one system for women, although there were similar kinds of work that both sexes did and were expected to do. Women predominated in household labor both in relationship to the slaveowner's house and their own household. Depending on the size of the plantation and its enslaved population, both men and women did field labor and outdoor maintenance in the appropriate seasons—road repair, planting, the cultivating and harvesting of crops, wood chopping, provision ground gardening, driving horse teams, and fence building or repair. Clearly women engaged in childbearing, rearing, and care in the midst of their other work regimens, although these activities were often assigned to enslaved older children or elderly slaves. The result of this kind of regimen is that enslaved women continually worked, from sunrise until past sunset.

In each era of slavery, the sex ratio became an issue in the work regimen. In the colonial period, there was a disproportionate number of enslaved men to women, in part because slaveholders were slow in realizing the potential for fecundity, and hence, for slave reproduction/work force increase. They focused instead on the need for male enslaved labor to clear and cultivate the wilderness. Potential female fecundity became an issue when the U.S. government banned the importation of slaves in 1808. The slave population had to increase naturally instead of depending on new enslaved Africans or smuggled enslaved Afro-Caribbeans. During the mature era of antebellum enslavement, and particularly during the Civil War, the number of male enslaved who became fugitives, Union volunteers, or plantation deserters altered the work regimen and responsibilities of the remaining enslaved women.[19]

The experience of enslaved female sexuality has been analyzed not only as to matters of population reproduction, but for stereotypes and myths of black female sexuality. Occurrences of rape, the existence of miscegenation laws, and black-white female social and work relations on plantations are areas where historians have discussed enslaved female sexuality. White analyzes the sexual and work myths of enslaved women as Jezebels on the one hand and asexual, pious, and pure "mammies" on the other hand. The contradiction of this dual image displays the need of planters for slave proliferation while also condemning the enslaved woman for her own supposed licentiousness. White further analyzes the public nakedness that blackwomen (and blackmen) were forced to endure when on examination for sale on the auction block, and the particular medical maltreatment enslaved women received during pregnancy and postnatal periods. Thus, White emphasizes the public definition and discussion of enslaved women's sexuality in a revisionist and more accurate light than earlier depictions.

Another contribution of blackwomen's slave historiography and the narratives is the discussion of social relations between enslaved women and white slave mistresses. The narratives draw attention to the sexual double standard for white men in relation to their wives and to their enslaved women. This double standard regarded the enslaved woman as inferior to the ideal Victorian female standard, but then judged her in light of those very same social standards. This victimization is illustrated in narratives describing mistress abuse of enslaved women, especially household enslaved women, or children born of miscegenation. Also, endemic to the social and physical location of women who worked in the planters' homes were power struggles for loyalty to the slave master in competition with the slave mistress. Such antagonisms and torn loyalties often endangered the enslaved woman. In addition, there were conflicts regarding child care for the slaveholder's children, which took precedence over the needs for care, socialization, and protection of her own children.

Besides the theme of enslaved blackwomen's vulnerability and victimization, the narratives call attention to the resources African American women possessed in the enslaved women's network, made possible in part by the sexual division of labor in the slave work regime and in the slave quarter community. The network, supportive community, and mutual assistance took place through midwifery, collective cooking and laundering, child care, quilting, and reformations of African patterns of work and residential living for women and children. Other activities included shared work coverage for women not physically strong enough to meet their work or production quotas and spiritual leadership among themselves and for the slave quarter community.

Many of these activities formed the basis of enslaved women's resistance, sabotage, and insurrection related to the slave institution. Cooking could be a graphic expression of insurrection via murder by poisoning. Work slowdowns could be the source of renegotiated work conditions. Feeding runaway slaves provided sources of hope for a different, if distant, future of freedom. And herbal and root medicine could serve as abortificients, whereby enslaved blackwomen controlled their procreation as much as possible.

White, Jones, and others also use the journals of slave mistresses, sympathetic and otherwise, and references and stories from black male narratives to broaden our understanding of enslaved women's reality. Fanny Kemble's journal, Fredrika Bremer's writings, and the accounts of such notable free blackwomen as Charlotte Forten are illustrative of nonslave sources used by blackwomen historians.

The work of these historians and their utilization of enslaved women's narratives have been important in several crucial ways. It reminds others that the task of slave historiography should be to uncover, recover, and reclaim documentation of and from the *whole* enslaved community, male and female. Analysis and interpretation of the enslaved experience needs to consider methods which incorporate race, gender, class, and division of labor perspectives of enslaved blackpeople and of the institutions and structures of slavery. In doing so, slave historiography becomes a recovery of the achievements and failures of the entire community in its struggle to create itself in its own and African-inherited image.

The Slave Narrative as Sacred Text

Slavery is the event which gives rise to and organizes the kidnapped and enslaved African into the enslaved African American, and which introduces the African to modern European Christianity, predominantly Protestantism.[20] It is also the event in which the African-become-African American creates the African American Christian faith community, giving rise to a unique expression of the nature of God, of Jesus, and of the Holy Spirit. Slavery thus becomes a *generative hermeneutical* event. Through it, we come to see the power of religious faith for an oppressed people:

> The slaves' religious ceremonies emphasized and tightened the social bonds among people. In the religious meetings the people of the slave quarters gathered together to discuss the events of the day, to gain new strength from the communal reality to face their individual realities, to celebrate the maintenance of life in the midst of adversity, and to determine the communal strategies and tactics. Out of these meetings came the modern black church . . . [one of many] social institutions both for accommodation and for struggle.[21]

Put differently in the words of an enslaved woman:

> I'se saved. De Lord done tell me I'se saved. Now I know de Lord will show me de way, I ain't gwine to grieve no more. No matter how much you all done beat me and my chillen de Lord will show me de way. And some day we never be slaves.[22]

As we shall see, the work and labor of enslaved women (and men) became a contested location for the struggle between enslaved and slaveowner. If this is true (and I believe so), then Christianity became a contested site as well—a *religious* battleground between the slavocracy's attempt to define and control slaves, and the enslaved African/African Americans' self-definition of their own humanity and religious viewpoint. Seen in light of this struggle, the slave narrative has another crucial dimension. Slave and ex-slave testimony bear witness to the power of God's Spirit. Slave and ex-slave testimonies express the enslaved one's intimate relationship with Jesus, and her/his belief in the power of prayer. Slave and ex-slave testimony proclaims that the purpose of God was not and is not slavery, but freedom. It shows how enslaved African Americans acted daily and decisively, in both large and small ways, as moral agents in response to their religious conversion and commitment to God's call to faith and freedom.

The slave narrative has acted as sacred text within this African American religious tradition, and a productive reading of the texts leads one to see the experience of chattel slavery as fundamentally the organizing hermeneutical event[23] for the faith story and religious tradition of African American Christians. Their texts and testimonies relate to constitutive elements in African American experience, including the African roots of the African American Christian, the historical event of enslavement and the impact of the institution of slavery, the aural and oral text of the culture (the WPA and FWP narratives), and the repository of theological and ethical moorings for contemporary guidance and reflection by the black Christian community. My premise is that the nature of the text—its declarative and central point—is the historical encounter of African Americans with the institution of chattel slavery. This historical experience provides the occasion for the written and oral discourse—the slave narrative. This experience is concretized in the narrative and is reflective not only of the individual narrator, but also of the collective narration of the signified event over a prolonged period of time.

In a sense, slave narratives are among the earliest narrative literature of African Americans. Many of them, prior to being

written down, were actually told to those whom they first encountered when reaching a relatively safe haven north of the Mason
Dixon Line. Some narratives were also dictated while others were
written in interview form. Thus, behind many of these transmis-
sions are oral presentations that became written documents. In
both forms, narratives were the creation of a people telling a story
that incorporated fundamental understandings shared by enslaved
people throughout the antebellum period. It is this collective experiential nature of the narrative—oral and written in expressing
faith journeys, clandestine worship, fervent prayer, and ultimate
hopes lifted to God—which approaches "sacred text."

The model presented by biblical scholar Walter Harrelson is
helpful in considering sacred text.[24] Harrelson's goal is to establish features of Israelite biblical literature that combine to create a
tradition—a central core of fundamental understandings or
content that is more than a mere theme or set of motifs, and which
is detectable in a process of handing down. Furthermore, "it
should be possible to identify its basic themes, the motifs that
articulate the themes, the plot that emerges, and the tradition as
something to be received and handed down intact."[25] According
to Harrelson, the salient characteristics of a tradition are that:

> (1) it is received from others and transmitted further,
> especially from one generation to the next; 2) it has both
> form and content . . . remaining formal for purposes of
> retracing it; (3) it is the immediate property of a group or
> a community, that is, has a direct function for the people
> who transmit it; (4) it is "living," developing, malleable
> and only relatively stable; it can become changed and
> reinterpreted to meet the needs of its transmitters; (5) it is
> usually oral but can also be in written form as long as it
> fulfills the other criteria mentioned here, especially that
> of being able to develop and adapt; and (6) it tends to be
> cumulative and agglomerate.[26]

These features suggest a means of appropriating the notion of
sacred text for the slave narrative without claiming that it has the

same stature as the Christian scriptures. We are reminded that one of the African features retained by African Americans was that part of their religious worldview was a sense of the unity of the cosmos in which all was viewed as sacred. This understanding pervaded the life of the individual, both internally and externally, and was applied as well to the social and natural world. Hence, it makes sense that the enslaved understood him-and-herself in a universe alive with the power of God. Accordingly, ex-slave Carey Davenport reported that:

> When darkies prayed in slavery they darns't let the white folk know 'bout it or they beat them to death. When we prayed we turned a wash pot upside down to the ground to catch the voice. We prayed lots in slavery to be free and the Lord heard our prayer. We didn't have no song books, the Lord gave us songs. When we sing them at night 'round the fireplace it would be just whispering like . . . so the white folks not hear us. We would hum them as we wo'ked in [the quarter] in the field, walking to town.[27]

Compressed within this testimony are myriad theological meanings that witness to slavery days, the nature and necessity of dangerous worship in a so-called Christian country, and the unity of religious life in spite of the reality of slavery. An outstanding dimension of this testimony is the extent to which slaves would go in order to worship God. They faced beatings, even unto death. Another ex-enslaved woman, Ellen Butler, said it this way: "Massa never 'lowed us slaves to go to church . . . they done that way cause white folks didn't want slaves to pray."[28] This response of slaves is found throughout the antebellum period.

First and second generations of liberation and womanist theologians and ethicists have affirmed that before there was African American Christianity or "slave religion," there was black religion.[29] Black religion had its origins in the diverse antecedents of African traditional religion(s) and cosmology. Upon coming into contact with a different—that is, European—understanding of history, Africans fused highly developed beliefs and pervasive feelings about the ontological nature of spirituality with their new historical experience of enslavement and Christianity. Black religion, as such, has always been grounded in the imagination of an irrepressibly religious people concerning God, and simultaneously and equally, concerning justice for themselves and others. Liberation is arguably a fundamental character of black religion and African American Christianity.

With the slave narrative, liberation and womanist theologians dialogue with the religious testimony and history of blackpeople, the black church, and black culture. In doing so, black religious scholars "hear" the unique way that the narratives focus attention on several key aspects of "doctrinal," spiritual, and cultural transmission and process within a community under the constraints of chattel slavery. A foundational aspect of spiritual and cultural transmission is the theological and experiential talk about "the Spirit" within the narratives. It is seen as an empowering force, especially when one "enters into the Spirit." Such talk about the spiritual journey as "getting ligion" is descriptive of both the dimensions of religious conversion and a release into the realm of God's freedom if not into physical freedom from bondage. An enslaved person narrated, "I kept on until I asked the Lord, if he had converted me, to show me a beautiful star out of a cloudy sky. This was done, and I saw a star in the daytime shining out of a cloudy sky. I know I have got it, and hell and its forces can't make me turn back."[30] Other narratives speak of "visions," "shouting," and "the slapping of hands" in the conversion experience. Such patterns indicated to the enslaved that they were human because they received the Spirit, and indicated that they were other than their owners' animals and property.

A related element that becomes a critical hermeneutical principle is that of the enslaved community as a community of resistance. Resistance is used broadly to illustrate a range of activities from the sabotage of the slaveowner's goods or will to outright insurrection. The narratives illustrate the manner in which enslaved people created "a way of life" that was able to distinguish between the false presentation of the "slave" self in the presence of whites, and an authentic black self displayed in the presence of one's enslaved bondmen and bondwomen. For example, Riggins Earl believes that the narratives express the moral agency of slaves in need of freedom and literacy as constituent elements in God-created-being-ness—that is, "the more the enslaved defied masters' authority in the name of freedom, the closer they were to becoming autonomous moral agents."[31] Thus, while the purpose and identity of a slave to one's owner was that of property and as a tool of labor, the narratives remind us that the enslaved utilized strategies and mechanisms to be moral agents, to be faithful to their understanding of God and God's authority.

Another aspect embedded in the narratives and related to the moral agency of resistance is the central feature of prophetic and solidarity discourse. Religious language is used by enslaved men and women to speak God's judgment on enslavement, to turn Christian slave ideology into a discourse of freedom using biblical imagery, and to build eschatological hopes whether on this side of death or beyond. One such example comes from Harriet Tubman when she gained her freedom in the North: "I looked at my hands to see if I was de same person now I was free. Dere was such a glory ober the fields, and I felt like I was in heaven."[32]

Slavery is the event out of which sacred witnesses to God arise and the event out of which sacred text, the slave narrative, is created. In 1975, James Cone wrote that "the story was both the medium through which truth was communicated and also a constituent of truth itself. In the telling of a truthful story, the reality of liberation to which the story pointed was also revealed in the actual *telling* of the story itself."[33] This shows how important slave narratives are as a critical source for the historical grounding of blackpeople's voices in oppression and struggle for African American theologians' and ethicists' constructive task and liberatory praxis. The vast majority of contemporary black and womanist theologians and ethicists affirm that "the black church [and black religion] begin in slavery . . . and thus slave religion provides the first source for a contemporary statement on black theology."[34] The slave narrative, as blackpeoples' story of slavery and blackpeoples' voice in faith and struggle, tells us how the enslaved defined their humanity and their religion.

Womanist Theo-ethics and the Slave Narratives

Just as the blackwomen slave historians have challenged the gender bias of both black and white male historians in interpretation of the slave narratives, womanist theologians and ethicists[35] have argued against gender bias of black male colleagues in their use of the slave narrative. Similar to the Bible, the slave narrative is as much a gendered sacred text as it is a historical, political, and socio-linguistic text. That is, the slave narratives are gendered writings which reveal the enslaved ones' thoughts, language, politics, theology, and ethics as women and men wrestling with the social constructions of gender in their times. They are narratives written in voices that are gendered voices and represent real people who suffered the degradation of slavery not only as African Americans, but also as socially defined female and male beings. Those narrative sources produced by and about enslaved women define the enslaved experience of the African American community as that experience profoundly affected the nature of womanhood, the understanding of relationship to God-Jesus-Holy Spirit, and the means and choices discerned by enslaved women in realizing human wholeness and freedom.

Womanist theological and ethical praxis endeavors to speak of a multidimensional tradition within African American Christianity. It is a perspective that seeks a position within the black church tradition and community, and in the academy. It challenges these traditions in light of the real lived experiences of African American women as theological subjects, thinkers, and moral agents, and in light of the dynamics of internalized racism, sexism, and patriarchal heterosexism, as well as classism. As part of the work of discovery, recovery, critical examination, and authentication of blackwomen's lives, womanist theologians and ethicists utilize slave narratives to demonstrate the nature of African American women's contemporary and historic religious experience and communal survival.

For womanist theo-ethicist thinkers, historicity and hermeneutics must begin with blackwomen's existence in and experience of slavery. Utilizing slave narratives, each author describes and analyzes the social condition of the enslaved women's existence—religious, legal, social, economic, and moral. Common to most is enslaved blackwomen's use of the Bible.

Jacquelyn Grant appropriates the slave narratives to demonstrate four points:

1. the Bible was the major source for the religious validation of blackwomen's lives (in opposition to the definition of them as "chattel," and in white Christian slave ideology as "heathen");
2. the Bible, as heard by blackwomen, gave blackwomen a "God-consciousness" commensurate and complementary to their conversion experiences;
3. the Bible made Jesus real as a co-sufferer who identified with them through undeserved suffering even though he was divine, and that he meant freedom to them as well; and
4. there was more to life than slavery or the cross—that is, resurrection.[36]

Grant cites such narratives as that of Sojourner Truth and ex-slaves' interviews from the WPA Federal Writers' Project.

Katie G. Cannon agrees that the Bible was the highest source of authority in enslaved women's lives and in the historic experience of blackwomen, and not the slaveholder or white Christian interpretations of the Bible. Cannon sees "black women's consciousness as the interpretive principle" which helps African American women to identify "texts and contexts," including the Bible and its characters, as they hold onto life in the face of oppression and death.[37] Scripture is searched for examples of how women in the Bible acted as models for enslaved women. A key theme for

Cannon is that the Bible presented for enslaved women—and presents for contemporary blackwomen—times and models of unpredictability (of both oppression and freedom) and therefore empowerment. Cannon calls this hermeneutical principle "surviving the blight."[38]

Delores Williams, as a theologian, demonstrates through her analysis of the Genesis character Hagar, the Egyptian and slave woman, that African American women recognize the female activity in the Bible as survival activity. She illustrates this thesis through an analysis of reproduction, motherhood, and surrogacy as they relate to blackwomen's understandings of the Bible. Williams sees womanist theology as a corrective to traditional black liberation and feminist theologies,[39] and also as a corrective to the emphasis in Grant and Cheryl Sanders on atonement as Jesus' major salvific role. She critiques the necessity of Jesus' divine "surrogacy" death on the cross as an oppressive biblical hermeneutic for blackwomen.

In light of each author's use of slave narratives, and their relation to blackwomen in each historic era, Cannon and Williams further recognize slave narratives as "sacred texts" which illumine the history, survival, God consciousness, and divine identity of African American women and their communities. For Cannon and Williams, then, slave narratives function in a fashion similar to the Bible, revealing how blackpeople have seen themselves and their history as a religious history and as a struggle for freedom, much like the divine drama of the Bible. As sacred texts, slave narratives provide a "faith naming" of the black experience in contrast to that of white Christian slave ideology and its legal structures. Instead of identifying with the naming by whites—"heathen," "brood sow," "work ox,"[40] "breeders," "Jezebels," chattel acquisitions, animals, property, or commodities—African American women could see themselves as "Sojourner Truth" and Harriet Tubman, "the Moses of her people."

Cannon, in her "Slave Ideology and Biblical Interpretation,"[41] addresses those texts to which slave narratives as sacred texts stand in opposition—that is, "the hermeneutical distortions of white Christians" in the antebellum period. She correlates the slave apologists' ideological and social commitments with their use of the Bible. She identifies this as hegemonic exegesis for social control and domination that was directed at morally and spiritually dis-empowering enslaved African Americans through racist mythology. Included in such racist mythology was:

1. the denial of African and African American peoples' humanity;

2. the Christian conversion and civilizing of the heathen, the curse of Ham, divinely sanctioned slavery, and the "great chain of being";

3. the revision of history and God's action in it—the predestination of Africans for slavery and white control of them according to God's will; and

4. the absence of a specific biblical injunction against slavery.

Each of these myths was based, according to Cannon, on the white slave apologists' understanding of the infallibility of the Bible. This in-depth ethical critique by Cannon is preeminent among the womanist theologians and ethicists in its construction of the use of slave narratives for womanist religious study.

The implications for using slave narratives in the praxis of womanist theologians and ethics are multidimensional. This approach places the experience of African American women in historic, theological, ethical, and socioeconomic relationship to their experience of oppression and struggle for liberation in the United States. In doing so, Grant, Cannon, Williams, and others examine resources for contemporary blackwomen. Grant and Williams call attention to the role blackwomen have played in the history of the black church and in liberation theology. They point to the oppression of blackwomen in the church and in society as parallel dynamics. Cannon and Williams name specific historical categories and characterizations which have affected black-women's personal and social identity—surrogate, work animal, and breeder—and replaced them with blackwomen's self-under-standing as theologians and moral agents—mothers of the community, agents of "quiet grace and unshouted courage."[42] Grant has taken steps, along with Cannon, Williams, and Riggs, to

explore through the narratives even the historically silenced
dimensions of class and its effects on blackwomen historically.
However, these raise up recovered and new hermeneutical principles in biblical and blackwomen's literary tradition as well as call
attention to historic characterizations of blackwomen.

Located in a different place within womanist ethical thought,
Cheryl Sanders, however, seriously doubts whether appropriating
a secular womanist framework to understand blackwomen's
authority, naming, ecclesial relationship, and spirituality is consistent with the experience of African American women in the
church.[43] Sanders argues that the definition of womanist created
by Alice Walker is problematic for blackwomen. For example, she
finds that Walker's understanding of "womanish" may undermine
the authority of mothers and other blackwomen adults in the eyes
of blackgirls who try and emulate the everyday wisdom of blackwomen that comes through adult women's experience. Sanders
seems to think that, in a time when parents are struggling to maintain authority and discipline with their children and teenagers,
womanism condones challenges to authority which are necessary
to the maintenance of blackfamilies as advocated by traditional
black Christian values. Furthermore, Sanders cautions that Christian womanists who opt for Walker's understanding of blackfemale
identity must scrutinize all of Walker's definition and not pick and
choose from among the meanings. This is particularly true for
Sanders, who sees Walker's definition of sexuality as detrimental
for blackwomen, for the blackfamily, and for the traditional values
of Christian-sanctioned heterosexuality. Nevertheless, each author
wrestles with the tasks and meaning of womanist thought for
interpreting the lives of contemporary African American women,
a group that is central in shaping U.S. society, beginning with the
origins of slavery itself.

In interpreting the slave narratives, it is important to identify
several implications for the conjunction of African American liberation theology and ethics with the interpretation of the slave testimonies, especially from womanist perspectives. First, notions of
faith, personal and collective liberty, and economic status are the-
matically related because "the slaves' faithful story about freedom

helps to unleash the full power of African American speech, which plums the depths of God's grace of freedom to the black poor."[44] Within the slavocracy, slaves had no voice with which to make and give speech except in compliant response to the demands and wishes of the slaveowner and the larger white society. This was particularly true for enslaved women and their children. To speak, particularly in religious language, autobiographies, interviews, and other genres, testifies to a counter-practice of power and consciousness. Enslaved women's use of religious language marks the joining of spirituality, theology, and moral agency. It is to insert, in a supposedly nonexistent space, the core of what it means to be human, which is personhood.

Second, the challenge to African American theology and ethics emerges in utilizing and clarifying the relationship between the living ancestral slave voices of the past, and the adaptation to and transformation of a white supremacist Christianity. What do the voices of slaves, pronouncing a liberating Christ, have to do with strategies and options for moral agency for the enslaved, then and now? How do the words and actions of enslaved women redefine the liberating Christ for blackwomen then and today?

A third consideration, already implied in the second, requires a risk-taking openness on the part of black Christian scholars to that part of the African American experience—enslaved and contemporary—which was and remains spiritual and religious, but not Christian. How does the desire for freedom and liberation by our enslaved ancestors inform the claims of black Christianity and our moral agency in light of our African traditionalist heritage, as well as our relationship with the wider African Diaspora and other Third World liberation struggles, Christian and otherwise?

Fourth, the slave testimonies speak of suffering, pain, and evil. For African American theologians and ethicists, the slave narratives challenge any easy theodicy, any easy notion of redemptive suffering or moral agency as we seek to understand a multifaceted expression of faith and life that seeks to be whole.

Finally, the community of slaves—their struggle and their voice—was communal even when expressed in and through individual testimony. Liberation ethics and theology is challenged to continuously reflect on the communal nature of our scholarly work and our accountability to the voices of the ancestors, the black church, and the black liberation struggle[45]—both male and female.

In-depth investigation of each of these implications is impossible in this book. However, many of them will be taken up in subsequent chapters pertaining to enslaved women's experience of work and implications for our contemporary situation. As I will show in chapter 2, the relationship between an African American and womanist liberation perspective is noteworthy in deciphering the nature of "religious capital" in the power struggle between enslaved people and slaveholders theologically and ideologically. Further, in chapter 3, this relationship becomes the critical hermeneutical framework for directly interpreting the work ethic of enslaved women through their own narratives. In doing so, the nature of the slave narrative as sacred text and source for moral reflection will become evident.

2

Tools of the Trade:
Methods in Constructing an Enslaved
Women's Work Ethic and Moral Agency

The reason for the establishment of African slavery in the New World was the need for a cheap labor source to build the infrastructure of an Atlantic European colonialism and capitalist market. It began in 1502. This historic development gave rise to what would become the objective structure and social relations called chattel slavery. After three and a half centuries of slavery, historians estimate that some 9,900,000 Africans were coerced into slavery.[1] The North American slave trade was never as substantial as that of the Caribbean and Latin America, although later, "the United States would become the leading slave power in the Western world."[2] The Atlantic slave trade came to North America in 1619 with the settlement of the British colony of Virginia, where a shipment of twenty black Africans landed. There, a mixture of Africans, free British wage laborers, and English indentured servants provided the colony's labor system. This system permitted the production of tobacco and indigo as export cash crops, and general farming for local consumption in the newly established colonies.

Historians of United States slavery and white racial attitudes point to unique features that propelled British colonial economic development as distinct from the remainder of European colonial expansion into the Western hemisphere. According to Stanley Elkins, "The New World had been discovered and exploited by a

European civilization which had always, . . . placed a high premium on personal achievement, and it was the special genius of Englishmen, from Elizabeth's time onward, to transform this career concept . . . into one of economic fulfillment."[3] Elkins goes on to explain that the Virginia colony, in particular, was established on "purely capitalistic incentives . . ."[4] by those who understood the possibilities of risk-taking in trade and production unavailable to them in Britain. Historian David Bertelson adds that nationalism was a factor that also propelled British colonial economic expansion. He claims, "Men were confident about the prospects of Virginia because these rested upon the conjunction of personal opportunity with the glory of God and the honor of the realm."[5] According to these historians, English colonial development emerged from the desire for more personal freedom and a restless, growing discontent with the more aristocratic forms of English social life. These desires were joined with the necessity to create new forms of English law, business practices, and the economics of cheap land in North America. These were the formative economic conditions that spawned the settlement of North America colonies for capital investment and profit.

During the first segment of North American slavery, from 1619 to 1680, most slaves were engaged in general farming and domestic occupations. Slave labor for tobacco production was steadily increasing. It was in this period that a three-tier system of labor in the North American British colonies provided the backdrop for institutionalized chattel slavery, and founded the political and moral economy of colonies like Virginia and Maryland. Besides slavery, free wage labor and indentured servitude were foundational to settlements in these colonies. These forms of non-slave labor were not identical. Both were based on contractual agreements, and both permitted the populating of colonies with British citizens.

Indentured servitude was a temporary contract in which British settlers (and other white ethnic Commonwealth groups such as the Welsh, Scots, and Irish) served in the employ of a master for a period of four to seven years, or in the case of legal minors, until age twenty-one. Indentured service was payment for their travel from England to North America. As part of the contract, an indentured servant could be sold or have his or her contract transferred from one master to another. This contract was mutually binding, with mutually reciprocal obligations. The indentured servant was under obligation to perform any and all labor. And the master was obliged to feed, clothe, punish but not abuse, and sometimes educate the servant. During the tenure of indentured servitude in the colonies, conditions for this labor were changed for the better by legislative fiat, often limiting maximum terms of indenture, specifying basic human needs to be met and fees to be paid upon expiration of the contract. The latter enabled the newly released to avoid immediate indigence. Such legislation created a stable environment where the need for labor was so great that incentives could mediate between the harshness of the system and the temptation to flee from service.[6]

The emergence of chattel slavery was directly linked to indentured servitude. Winthrop D. Jordan asserts that in Virginia and Maryland colonies, chattel slavery developed along different lines than it did in New England, New York, New Jersey, and Pennsylvania colonies. In the former, the need for labor was of a specific nature, given capital investment in any cash crop exportation. With a labor shortage and the abundance of land to be cultivated, indentured servitude was too temporary and expensive, given the required long-term capital investment. Moreover, community-related commitments, such as religious freedom, as found in most New England colonies, were generally absent. Jordan remarks that in New England, "there was no compelling economic demand for Negroes [as evidenced] in the numbers actually imported: economic exigencies scarcely required the establishment of a distinct status for only three-percent of the labor force."[7]

This perspective is further elaborated by David Brion Davis, but with an additional insight into New England's role in the institutionalization concerning slavery. According to Davis, "It is a fact that slavery became legal in all the English colonies and that trade in that commodity became an economic mainstay in New

England."[8] Thus, while colonies like Maryland, Virginia, and South Carolina imported Africans as slave labor for the development of staple cash export crops, New England states traded slaves to the South as part of its own economic base.

According to McGary and Lawson, "as early as 1604, some owners adopted the practice of considering blacks, and the children of bound black women, slaves for life, even before it became part of the official legal system." (This was a practice later to be codified into law as *partus sequitur ventrem*—the child follows the condition of the mother.[9] Such a practice ensured that enslaved women would become valued for their reproductive capacities as well as being valued targets for rape, concubinage, and sexual liaisons for slaveholders, their sons, and their overseers. The enslaved were legally considered property, real and chattel (personal), as evidenced by various colonial statutes after 1660 in Virginia, Maryland, New York, New Jersey, South Carolina, Pennsylvania, and Rhode Island.[10]

Jordan reports that during the same period, other slaveholding practices were being codified which relegated Africans and African Americans to an anomalous social status: "Virginia law set Negroes apart from all other groups . . . by denying them the important right and obligation to bear arms. Few restraints could indicate more clearly the denial of membership to Negroes in the white community."[11] From 1650 onward, colonies began codifying moral and legal restrictions for interracial sexual relations and marriage.

In the eighteenth century, colonies began to enact additional legislation requiring newly freed slaves to leave their territories (North and South Carolina) or laws even prohibiting all manumissions except those granted for meritorious service (Virginia). In other colonies, laws were diverse. In New York, free blacks were immune in court from testimony given by slaves, while in New England slaves could testify against anyone.[12] Most colonies also prohibited blacks from service in the militia, or from voting in public elections, or from participation in government lotteries. With the ratification of the United States Constitution, the compromise between the creation of slave and free states by way of congressional representation solidified chattel slavery as an objective structure within the new democracy. Thus, the development of slavery as an objective economic, political, and agricultural structure, and the actions of those in control of those structures, provides one framework for understanding the "peculiar institution."

Foundations of Moral Agency

The slave narratives are vehicles for interpreting the slaves' response to their own condition as created by these structures of hegemony. When I speak of the response of enslaved people to slavery, I am fundamentally speaking about "moral agency." I find the discussion of moral agency by social ethicist Peter Paris helpful in defining the nature of this most humanlike capacity. Paris states that moral agency is

> [T]he capacity to determine the quality of human activity by making choices in accordance with understandings of good and bad, right and wrong. As moral agents, human beings are able to perceive others as subjects, and in their encounter with them they may choose to treat them either as subjects or as objects . . . Morality is born only in the act of treating the other as a person, since to do otherwise would be an objectification of the other: hence destruction of the other's personhood, and not only that but also a corresponding loss of the agent's own personhood.[13]

This understanding of moral agency assumes that morality is *always* a social activity, as is being a moral agent. The moral realm of human life is a reciprocating dynamic in which the moral act ("doing") itself is what makes the human a person ("being"). Moral activity, according to Paris, is "social" because it is always activity that takes place in relation to other persons. The result is that moral activity is never a private or "socially isolated" activity.[14]

Furthermore, Paris' notion of moral agency assumes a certain understanding of the nature of the person-in-society. That is to say, persons are related to their socio-economic-political-cultural-religious contexts in an organic way: Existence is mutually (although not equitably) dependent. As persons, we are different from society just as society is equally different from all its individual members in total. In fact, society is more than the sum total of all its members, constituting a human reality that transcends the individual. Yet, the person and society are interrelated because the society is both the necessary and the sufficient means for human development. Even our personal faith understanding and community are shaped socially within a context of a basic set of shared values and corporate existence—the ethos of the society— its most pervasive and deep cultural beliefs, symbolic practices, and expectations. It is the collective response of a group arising from and organizing its understanding of life.

Related to a people's ethos is their worldview: the way in which a people make sense of their surroundings, their life, and the universe. It is the explanatory schema behind why particular groups do the things in the world that they do. A people's world-view—customs, rituals, patterns of organization—determine a group's perceptions of the structure of the self, nature and the universe, and what we know as constituting "truth," "knowledge," and reality.[15] Together, a people's ethos and worldview are the building blocks of their culture, and provide its understanding of their personal identity, group accountability, and corporate mission or purpose. Thus, morality and agency are socially grounded in ethos and worldview. In the case of chattel slavery, both slaveholders and the enslaved had their respective ethos and worldviews within the larger social worlds that they inhabited.

The moral agency of antebellum enslaved blackwomen in relation to work and human meaning occurs within the web of the objective, historical structures of slavery, the everyday experience of these structured relations, and the ethos and worldviews which respectively shape the enslaved and slaveholders. In this social world, slaveholders are not only persons acting as moral agents who dominate the enslaved but also as occupants of constructed positions of power and interests within that world. Likewise, the enslaved are not only persons also acting as moral agents and a group who are dominated, but are also occupants of constructed positions of less power, and yet who nevertheless maintain their own interests as well.

These different yet related ethos, worldviews, and objective relations are embedded in the social world. These worldviews are interactive and possess as well a dimension that functions relatively autonomously at times. They include constructed worldviews about the racial self/community, the religious self/community, the gendered self/community, and economic work-related self/community. These worldviews have different cultural and geographical points of origin, which affect their adaptation and transformation in the British North American colonies and later in the United States. West and Central African common orientations undergirded the African American enslaved community, while a western European and North American ethos and worldview structured objective relations in producing particular constructs of race, religion, gender, and work. For these reasons, a multidimensional, theoretical, and methodological framework seems appropriate in this undertaking.

Methods for Revealing the Madness of Slavery

Theoretically speaking, the operation of slavery, and the structured agency of persons within it, is the subject of this chapter. My task is to present a framework that expresses the multidimensional (although not necessarily mutual) nature of the social world of slavery and of enslaved moral agency within it. To do this, I make use of four theoretical and methodological perspectives. The first two perspectives are specifically African American–centered ones: the notion of African common orientations, and a womanist liberation ethical methodology for situating the world of black-women, and especially enslaved blackwomen. These two perspectives understand African American and blackwomen's existence from the dimension of resistance to oppression, the struggle for freedom, and the self-determination of African American quality of life. Then I theorize the social world institutional slavery in terms of hegemony, drawing upon Pierre Bourdieu's post-structuralist "logic of practice"—the ideas of "field," "practice," *"habitus,"* and "distinction." Lastly, I turn to James C. Scott's analysis of the "hidden transcript" (those practices masked from the view of the dominating public) to correct a view of action that I believe remains overdetermined in Bourdieu's construction of objective structures.

It has been noted earlier that the enslaved African American woman's experience and understanding of work was conditioned by the objective reality of slavery and also by the dynamic adaptation of Christianity by the enslaved. In the theoretical and methodological constructions used here, I assume that the objective structures of slavery, and certainly those of Christianity, were value-laden structures given the notions of ethos and worldview I have discussed. I hold the same assumption about the enslaved African American existence, structured as it was by African common orientations—that is, that they too are value-laden objective relations influencing the attitudes of enslaved women and the community of the enslaved.[16] This assumption is fundamental to the whole enterprise of discerning an enslaved woman's work ethic. It asserts that those structures, as well as persons, are the bearers of values and that, in fact, the relation between persons and structures is a highly charged, reciprocal, and dynamic process of creating, maintaining, and transforming the world.

Furthermore, I have chosen a Eurocentric framework in which to understand, in part, enslaved blackwomen's action-attitudes about work because their social world was constructed from more than an African worldview and from more than one set of objective relations. It was a world created and maintained by certain material conditions and assumptions having their origins and dynamic interplay within European economic, political, social, gender, and religious and racial social worlds. In seeking to understand the production of meaning and agency regarding human labor for enslaved women, the social world must be investigated from theoretical and methodological perspectives that adequately problematize the nature of that social world. Religious, and specifically Protestant, social ethics must not only use the "theo-ethical tools"[17] by which it understands the production of meaning, but it must also use the tools of the social sciences to disclose more fully that particular meaning and value produced within the logic and operations of the social world as a multidimensional, and not just religious, reality.

African Common Orientations

I have contended, with black theologians and ethicists, how slave testimonies speak in the religious voice of the enslaved. We have asserted that slave narratives are sacred text which function as the organizing story and hermeneutic for the African American tradition within the "invisible institution." Given these affirmations, one must ask how African Americans "came to religion." What is the grounding of this religious voice and from whence did it come? To understand the religious voice and moral agency of the enslaved, one must explore the cultural ethos and worldview that shaped the development of the African American religious self. It is arguably true that enslaved (and free) Africans began a process of cultural transformation when they became enslaved Africans and African Americans in the New World. That is, Africans in America created a new yet interrelated New World African culture by using common and diverse traditional African ethos and worldviews in a dynamic process as a result of having to reconstitute a new human sociality within, and as a response, to enslavement.

I suggest that African American culture, and particularly spirituality, is the foreground in African traditional culture and spirituality. Culture, as I have proposed, is anchored in the ethos and worldview of a people that is a fluid interaction of three phenomena:

1. subjective constructions of behavior, belief, and thought;
2. formal structures of collective behavior, belief, and thought; and
3. the everyday practices of living.

These elements are what Clifford Geertz calls "the imaginative universe" of familiarity or "the powerful, pervasive, and long-lasting moods and motivations" of a people.[18] Such "moods and motivations" adhere in both the culture as a whole and in its members. One example is the "slave marriage ritual." Despite the law and their status as chattel property, women and men in the enslaved community were disposed to marriage and to families not unlike those of the Euro-American model. Often such relationships were communally ritualized in ceremonies like the widespread "jumpin' the broom," *a ritual of unknown origin except within the enslaved community.*[19] Contrary to white people's construction of slave religion, marriage, and family, subversive communal patterns modeled relational practices that gave stability to enslaved life. Fred Brown, an ex-slave from Baton Rouge, recalled, "Den sometimes a couple am 'lowed to git married and dere am extry fixed for supper. De couple steps over de broom laid on de floor, dey's married den."[20]

Since persons experienced the Middle Passage and not "societies," Africans from diverse cultures and ethnic groups began forging connections using the shared elements of African traditional ontological, epistemological, cosmological, and sociological frameworks even before their arrival in the New World. Social historian Sterling Stuckey claims that "during the process of their becoming a single people, Yorubas, Akans, Ibos, Angolans, and others were present on slave ships to America and experienced a common horror . . . As such, slave ships were the first real incubators of slave unity across cultural lines, cruelly revealing irreducible links from one ethnic group to the other."[21] Individuals found ways of expressing and sharing with one another those elements of their societies that were mutually recognizable, and they molded them in new ways for a new situation, even without the institutional or structured forms that we commonly call culture.

Thus the phenomenon of transformation—transmission, re-creation, and socialization—may have had more to do with socio-relational necessities than with particular practices per se. A dynamic movement, transformation is not a process of transferring "one-to-one correspondences" from African ethnic groups to enslaved African Americans; it is seeing the cultural diversity in its overarching framework. Molefi Kete Asante best makes the point:

> Africa is one cultural river with numerous tributaries characterized by their specific responses to history and environment. In this way we have seen Europe after the Christian manifestations [become] one culture although at the same time they were different . . . [Thus] Asante, Yoruba, Mandinka, are also one, though different in the historical sense.[22]

From the perspective of a traditional African philosophical framework, what I call African common orientations[23] provide the foreground for the religiosity and spirituality of enslaved African Americans. In making this claim, I am not only suggesting the "powerful moods and motivations" of an African heritage were transformed for the survival of a people and the creation of a culture; I am also affirming that the enslaved did not become *tabula rasa*—the total victims of the dominant enslaving culture. Instead, the enslaved became active agents in resisting dominant forms, creating new forms, and appropriating and transforming Euro-American cultural forms. This point is forcefully made by anthropologists of religion Karen McCarthy Brown and Roger Bastide. Brown asserts:

> . . . that the slave diaspora had the effect of separating the "world of symbols, collective representations, and values from the world of social structures and their morphological bases." In [Bastide's] view the process by which . . . systems moved into the New World consisted of a search for the appropriate social "niches" in which symbolic representations could survive. In some cases . . . such niches were found. In others they were not.[24]

The remarks by Brown and Bastide illustrate an important position. "Systems" did move into the New World through individuals. However, it is crucial to recognize that systems had to find "niches"—hiding places amenable to African cultural interpenetration—in the dominant structures of Euro-American culture in order to be transformed by, and useful to, enslaved people. Will Coleman's work on slave religion and non-Christian experiences with the Spirit provides an example of such niches and interpenetration. A belief in spirit-beings, ghosts, and haunts as representations (symbolic forms) of mutually reciprocating relations between living and dead ancestors (kinfolk) was a deep socioreligious system embedded in the spirituality of many enslaved women and men. As slaves encountered Eurocentric Christianity, such experiences as visions and dreams as well as that of the Holy Spirit were appropriated into slave religion and into Christian faith. "Grammaw," a WPA generation, ex-enslaved woman, recounted, "When I been converted, I went to Hebben in de sperrit an' see wid de eye of fait. I done been there . . ."[25] Coleman claims that slave religion was an "organic syncretism that enabled slaves to combine their African-centered beliefs with the Eurocentric ones of their masters." African American Christianity was the result.[26]

Yet, when necessary, African patterns of religious instruction and practice stood on their own—that is, fully structured and revealed in persons and groups. For example, the religious instruction acquired in an enslaved woman's quarters undergirded the structuring of religious experience as it had taken place in everyday life for women and children in many African societies. WPA interviews related that "The Negroes on plantations sometimes appoint one of their number, commonly the old woman who minds the children during the day to teach them to say their prayers, repeat a little catechism and few hymns every evening."[27] Also, the religious practices, no matter how varied, undergirded the structuring of future hopes, aspirations, and experiences. Rebecca Grant, an ex-enslaved woman, reported, "My mother, all de time she'd be prayin' to the Lord. She'd take us chillun to de woods to pick up firewood, and we'd turn around to see her down on her knees behind a stump, a-prayin'. We'd see her wipin' her eyes wid de corner of her apron—first one eye, den de other as we come along back. Den, back in de house, down on her knees, she'd be a-prayin'."[28] Even more poignantly, Ellen Butler recalls, "Marster neber 'low he slaves to go to chu'ch. Dey hab big hole out in de fiel's dey git down in and pray. Dey done dat way 'cause de white folks didn't want 'em to pray. De uster pray for freedom. I dunno how dey larn to pray, 'cause dey warn't no preachers come roun' to teach 'em. I reckon the Lawd jis' mek 'em know how to pray."[29] In the above quotations, the religious *habitus* is both individually and group structured. Simultaneously, that *habitus* structures the dispositions of the individual and group so that the group and its members can understand and respond to the enslaved condition with a resistance grounded in shared religious practices.

Without romanticizing the traditional African past and its movement into African American culture and religion, I presuppose several traditional African *religious* common orientations:

1. traditional African cosmology that understands the whole universe as sacred (inclusive of a Supreme Deity) and spirit filled (inclusive of matter), without a dichotomy of the "sacred" and the "mundane," and that is the source and preserver of all life;[30]

2. the goal of traditional African morality, which is "to live life robustly"[31] with the life force of the universe, the Deity, and the ancestors and the family, especially children;

3. the centrality of the communal in persons, including right relationship and responsibility in regard to family, ancestors, the kin and ethnic group rather than a prominence of the individual person and will; and

4. a spirit of hospitality and a respect for difference.[32]

Furthermore, I presuppose three traditional African *philosophical* and *social* orientations:

1. female traditions of independence and responsibility as moral agents in different social structures;

2. gender complementarity and organization of communal patterns of sexual division of labor, political leadership, social, and economic life (which can be

found in both matrilineal and patriarchal groups); and

3. modes of association, analogy, ideas, and emotions (rather than abstracted reason and forms of dichotomy).

These African common orientations become vectors and patterns for uncovering broad continuums of cultural and religious roots of enslaved women as revealed in the slave narratives. And further, they assist in understanding the formation of blackwomen's moral agency in human labor.

A Womanist Framework and Methodology

Rooted in the definition of "womanist"[33] as articulated by Alice Walker, womanist theological and ethical perspectives focus on the experience of African American women. For the purpose of this discussion, a womanist framework functions as a lens or gaze by which African American women claim a particular part of the multifaceted and complex nature of the black experience in the United States. That lens organizes, analyzes, and articulates a blackwoman's self-understanding from the frames of blackness, femaleness, maleness, age, social and class location, and the historic struggle of blackwomen in community with blackmen and others for justice and freedom. That is, "womanist" is the African American experience as defined, contextualized, retrieved, envisioned, and celebrated in personal and communal spirituality as an empowering resource for the past, present, and future through blackfolk culture by *blackwomen*. Foundational to this lens is blackwomen's seeking liberation as full human beings from structural and personal forms of oppression. This liberation struggle takes into account and stands in relationship to the liberation struggles and hopes for justice of other peoples. Thus, my commonsense meaning of "womanist" is

1. a focus on the developmental process of becoming a blackwoman; that is, a focus on the movement from

childhood into the reality of responsibility and accountability of adult blackwomanhood;

2. a sociality of womanhood and a solidarity in which blackwomen can experience the full range of human emotion and personhood without being stigmatized or stereotyped;

3. an inquisitiveness about the ways of the world, and blackwomen's worlds specifically; a practical wonder toward and respect for the diversity yet interrelatedness of human beings;

4. an agency, particularly moral and cultural, that is a lifetime "work" for blackwomen;

5. a motherhood (biological and/or communal) lived out against white cultural and class-laden definitions and expectations of femininity;

6. an oppositional stance toward the personal, interpersona, cultural, and institutional forms of oppressions that affect one's health, relationships, racial identity, understanding of self as a sexual being, and capacity to act with intention and power in the world; and

7. a fundamental spiritual understanding of life that allows one to be empowered by remembering the history, the struggles of the present, and the visions for the future.

Womanists in religious studies assert that white feminist theory and method, history, ethics, and theology are inadequate to the task of explicating blackwomen's lives.[34] Jacquelyn Grant, addressing the topic of Christology, claims white feminist theology and ethics has limitations because its nature and sources are based, in reality, on white women's experience. This experience is radically different from that of blackwomen, beginning in slavery and proceeding through each historic era—Reconstruction, Jim Crowism, the Civil Rights Movement, and the post–Civil Rights era. Further, she claims that the nature of feminist theology and ethics is inherently racist, still defining blackwomen as racialized "other," and exclusive of the experience of blackwomen in its

method and analysis. Grant also maintains that feminist ethics and
theology falsely avow reconciliatory solutions while refusing to
examine the power relations of race and class. Grant, Cannon, and
Williams all recognize that feminist theology has contributions to
make in the interpretation of blackwomen's experience, and needs
to be in dialogue with womanist religious thought, but not without
seriously rethinking and engaging the historic experience of.
blackwomen.[35] As stated in the previous chapter, "emancipatory
historiography" becomes the critical hermeneutical principle for
investigating African American experience and, for womanist theologians and ethicists, African American women's lives in
enslavement.

Methodologically, this type of historiography and perspective
necessitates a womanist perspective that begins with making the
everyday, ordinary lives of blackwomen the center and departure
point for building theory. This theory is to be related specifically
to understanding the nature of the slave world, the humanity, and,
in the case of religious ethics, the moral agency of the enslaved
female. This means that the everyday actions, ideas, and life organization of blackwomen are the concrete foundations of theory.
By positively privileging these elements, blackwomen's experience becomes integral to the process of theorizing. This is the
opposite of most Western, academic developments of theory, in
that it openly states the particularized frame of reference for
"naming the world," that the frame of reference is blackwomen
and not white male and female experience universalized for all
people, and that it is unapologetic in doing so. Ethicist Cheryl
Sanders expresses this point of view:

> The fact that almost all of their [womanist] footnotes are
> derived from the writings of black women sends the
> important signal that we are appreciating the appropria-
> tion of our own sources, and also those of black men,
> without appealing for the most part, to white sources for
> sanction and approval of what we ourselves have said.
> This observation is especially significant in view of the
> fact that in a racist society, self-hatred manifests itself in
> the academy as in the ghetto when we are pressured to

employ our oppressors' criteria to evaluate our work and worth. To see black women embracing and engaging our material is a celebration in itself.[36]

In naming the world and the nature of humanity, therefore, a womanist perspective necessarily must address the issues that affect the lives of blackwomen, those things that negate the personhood of blackwomen and negate the black community. It is this negation of personhood that has been the core feature of blackwomen's lives in the United States. It takes the forms of white racist supremacy, misogyny, class, and cultural exploitation. These forms of oppression have continuously held African Americans—women and men—in the bind of a double standard, making them the objects of distorted definitions of personhood, while simultaneously holding them accountable to those distortions. This double standard has been built, in part, on notions of freedom, choice, and personal (sexual) morality and economics, as these constructs are defined in the dominant ethical systems of Western thought and Protestant Christian ethics.[37]

A womanist method and theory emerging from the lived experience of blackwomen unearths this double standard, which attacks the moral sensibilities of African American women. Katie G. Cannon first raised the challenge of womanist Christian, liberationist ethics against this double standard. She wrote:

> . . . the dominant ethical systems implied that the doing of Christian ethics in the Black community was either immoral or amoral. The cherished ethical ideas predicated upon the existence of freedom and a wide range of choices proved null and void in situations of oppression. The real-lived texture of Black life requires moral agency that may run contrary to the ethical boundaries of main line Protestantism. Blacks may use action guides that have never been considered within the scope of traditional codes of faithful living. Racism, gender discrimination, and economic exploitation, as inherited, age-long complexes, require the Black community to create and cultivate values and virtues in their own terms so that they can prevail against the odds with moral integrity.[38]

In addition, Cannon wrote:

> Dominant ethics also assumes that a moral agent is to a
> considerable degree free and self-directing . . . Due to
> extraneous forces and the entrenched bulwark of white
> supremacy and male superiority which pervade this
> society, Blacks and whites, women and men are forced to
> live with very different ranges of freedom.[39]

Thus by the standards of white racist supremacy, blacks have been
held inferior, and yet accused of an unwillingness to "pull themselves up by their bootstraps" like everyone else. In fact, very few
people in U.S. history have individually "pulled themselves up."
Upward mobility has been largely a function of varied caucasian
ethnic groups struggling to attain power—through politics,
unions, education, and so forth. Blackwomen have been judged by
the standards of white womanhood and found wanting. Yet they
have been fair game to the sexual and physical assaults of white
men. Until recently, as a class of workers with the legacy of
bondage as chattel, blackwomen have always been relegated to
the most demeaning work and employment statuses. They were
forced to nurture the children of whites, while being seen as the
most "liberated" of women, managing both work and family.
Blackwomen have been the "backbone" and the major con-
stituency of the black church, and they have been designated as
the most religious women in America. Yet their religious heritage
and traditions have been constantly described as "emotional" and
"primitive."

   Against this double standard is the affirmation of personhood
in the forms of community-building, kin and friendship ties, spirituality, dreams of equality, freedom and justice, and the celebration of collective ancestral ties to Africa, which have been the
sources of blackwomen's survival and aspiration. This affirmation
of personhood begins in each moment that blackwomen develop
the ability to see, understand, and tell the complexities and diver-
sities of the truth of African American women within the array of
black female difference, including their roles assigned by society.
In the face of white racist supremacy, affirmation of self becomes

an exorcism of both external hatred and internalized self-hate. The self constructs the struggle for positive valuing of womanhood from the intuitions, skills, and actions, and from the social relations with other women, which provide protection for the self and family against strategies designed to negate humanness.

A womanist methodological analysis and theoretical construction of an enslaved women's work ethic, based on the slave narratives, becomes an analysis of the discourse African American women create and use in thinking, acting, and rethinking the meaning of work. It posits as its analytic focus three significant dimensions that can be applied to both the objective relations and subjective relations in blackwomen's lives. These dimensions include: (a) the nature and interrelationship of social and work roles assigned to enslaved women, (b) the constructed justification of enslaved women's roles, and (c) the power relationships inherent in these roles which confront enslaved women. The overall womanist framework I use, "The Dance of Redemption," was developed by Katie G. Cannon, and has been a consistently reliable methodological guide in exploring blackwomen's lives and moral agency:

1. *conscientization:* awareness marked by "cognitive dissonance," i.e., when the experience of reality contradicts the normative understanding of reality;

2. *emancipatory historiography:* uncovering the systems or logic that hold the structures of oppression in place;

3. *theological resources:* discerning the theological doctrines and spiritual understandings that uphold or liberate structures of oppression;

4. *norms clarification:* deciphering values and norms operative within the community of accountability;

5. *strategic options:* identifying the options for action and their consequences that conscientization make possible;

6. *annunciation and celebration:* the recognition that change and liberating action is collective, not solely

individual, and collectively remembering, naming, and celebrating the presence and power that sustains struggle against oppression; and

7. *re-reflection/strategic action and conscientization:* the process begins again from the insights and learning of the previous struggle, yet at a new and deeper spiraling level.[40]

This womanist paradigm of emancipatory historiography and critical reflection is addressed not only to the objective character of blackwomen's oppression, but to its subjective character as well. For my purposes, it looks explicitly for enslaved blackwomen's moral agency and their reconstruction of the world in the context of oppression. It seeks a construction of an enslaved blackwomen's work ethic arising from the character and discourse of enslaved women's narratives.

I utilize this ethical method to understand the lives of enslaved women in relation to a constructive work ethic. I hypothesize that the departure point for this investigation includes two intersecting elements in the lives of enslaved women: (a) the encounter with conflicting Christian notions of a work ethic in the antebellum era, and (b) the struggle for emancipation from chattel slavery as a vital dimension in Christian moral agency. Furthermore, the encounter and the struggle are dynamics placed within a cultural legacy of African communal and religious sensibilities or common orientations. The first element, conflicting Christian notions of a work ethic, takes shape from the tension between "official Christianity" (imparted by the slaveholders and their wives, white preachers, and denominational or mission-related catechisms), and the subversive Christianity of the invisible institution, the "slave church." The second element displays itself in direct action by the enslaved to effect their own freedom, activities made manifest in slave narratives and the broader literature and records of black and white abolitionism. The third element, a cultural legacy of African communal and religious sensibilities or common orientations, is appropriated from historical research, cultural and religious anthropology, and the sociology of

religion. Albert Raboteau, Lawrence Levine, and others hold that
West and Central Africans had a heritage that "speaks of similar
modes of perceptions, shared basic principles, and common patterns of rituals . . . [with] enough fundamental similarities [to]
allow a general description of the religious heritage of African
slaves."[41]

The slave narrative sources produced by and about enslaved
women reveal the experience of the African American community
as that experience profoundly affected the construction of womanhood, the understanding of one's relationship to God-Jesus-Holy
Spirit, and the means and choices discerned by enslaved women in
realizing human wholeness and freedom. Thus a womanist method
is particularized and permits the recovery of the unique expression
of the nature of the human. In the case of an enslaved women's
work ethic, womanist methodology permits the investigation of
blackwomen's self-understanding of work unchained from
slavery's meaning, yet arising out of those very chains. Using the
womanist method, the "cognitive dissonance" of the moral ideal
and the moral reality of work that faced those who were enslaved
will become evident. The mythic stereotypes of white supremacy
regarding the enslaved work ethic are unmasked in light of
enslaved women's history, and the theological resources and
ethical norms upon which enslaved women drew are examined. A
complex relationship between moral action, faith, and reassess-
ment of life's meaning unfolds through the womanist prism.

A Logic of Practice

In light of the womanist standpoint perspective, Pierre Bourdieu's "logic of practice" theoretically and methodologically
assists one to understand the dynamic of reciprocating (although
not mutual) nature of the social relations of enslavement from the
perspective of the slavocracy. According to his theory, the social
world (or social reality) is relational, multidimensional, and interactive rather than simply objectively structured (naturally deter-
mined, given, and ahistorical) or subjectively structured (primarily
from individual will and interest). "It is a set of invisible relations,

those very same relations that constitute a space of positions exterior to each other and defined by their proximity to . . . or distance from each other, and also by their relative position . . ."[42] As such, it consists of the interrelated but relatively autonomous "fields" in which the human struggle for power takes place. It is a world that humans create, name, and interpret as meaningful so that humans can live without the necessity of repeating the process of re-creating this world continuously each time from the beginning. As part of the nineteenth-century social world, antebellum chattel slavery was a world of struggle between slaveholders and the enslaved—two classes or groups struggling over power as represented through the ownership of chattel, work and labor, religion, family and sexuality, and more abstractly, freedom.

In this framework, sociology and anthropology are usable tools for uncovering the normative, formative principles of operation of the social world, and how people act in an everyday and taken-for-granted manner—in this instance, the everyday world of slaveholders and enslaved women. For Bourdieu, the point is to understand (among other things) how objective structures, individuals, and groups within them function in relation to concrete class and status positions through forms of capital—economic, symbolic, cultural—in the "fields" of interrelated social space. Note that for Bourdieu, the term, *economy,* becomes the major metaphor for describing the nature of the social world and all its parts, not just the economic materialism of the marketplace.

Bourdieu's logic of practice is built on a framework of four conceptual tools. These are "fields," "practice," *"habitus,"* and "class." None of these concepts in themselves is unique, yet within Bourdieu's theory, they take on a new schematic relationship. These "tools" are useful for investigating the intersection of the objective relations of slavery as these tools affect the social world of enslaved women. In the manner of Bourdieu, I define "structures" or "objective relations" as the relations within which the regular and regulated material conditions characteristic of specific groups take place, structure, and generate the structuring practices and representations of the groups.[43]

Fields

In the social world, all human activity, or "world making," takes place between individuals and groups in "fields." A field, for Bourdieu, is defined as

> . . . a network, or a configuration, of objective relations between positions objectively defined, in their existence and in the determinations which they impose upon their occupants, agents or institutions . . . the structure of the distribution of power (or capital) . . . that [is] at stake in the field, as well as by their objective relation to other positions.[44]

The individuals and groups who participate in different fields seek to preserve or alter the form of capital appropriate to that field according to their interest or stake in the field. Since a social world is made up of various fields of struggle, the social world of slavery can be interpreted to have many such fields. On the one side, slaveowners seek to maintain the institution of slavery through fields that are relatively autonomous but clearly interrelated. For example, the "legal field" of chattel property is the slaveowner's ownership of the bodies of the enslaved. The "work or labor field" is related to the control and productivity of the work habits of the enslaved. Likewise, the "sexual and reproductive field" is the area of slave breeding which increases the enslaved work force reproductively (through breeding, sale, and trade), develops concubinage to meet their own sexual desires, and contests the ability of enslaved people to make their own choices of partners and families. Moreover, "the religious field" serves to sanctify slavery as the divine, patriarchal intent.

On the other side, the enslaved seek to gain their freedom legally or illegally within these and other fields. They seek to own their bodies, to control the ownership of their own labor or at least to modify their work regimes, to create and sustain their families, to worship God in their own way, and to interpret for themselves the will of God. By seeing the aims of slaveholders and the enslaved in this way, it is clear why "Bourdieu therefore assumes a fundamental link between actions and interests, between the practices of agents and the interests which they knowingly and unknowingly pursue, while at the same time rejecting the idea that interests are always narrowly economic."[45] Thus, fields organize a means of understanding the logic of the objective positions that slaveholders and the enslaved have in the social world of slavery. Fields also indicate the form of their interaction as agents, and the representations or "distinctions" (a concept to be discussed later) that distinguishes one class or group from another.

Since labor is the value being explored in this work for its meaning in the lives of enslaved women, I will illustrate the nature of labor as a field of struggle in the social world of slavery. From the 1831 plantation diary of slaveholder James Henry Hammond, historian Drew Faust reconstructs the following description:

> In the realm of labor, Hammond's desire for omnipotence was expressed in an unceasing pursuit of efficiency . . . The new owner found his laborers accustomed to task work, a system in which a clearly defined daily job was assigned to each hand. When this duty was completed, the slave's time was his or her own. Hammond regarded such arrangements as wasteful of the labor potential of his work force . . . Such a system, moreover, undermined . . . order, for it provided the slave too much autonomy and permitted hours of dangerous independence.[46]

What is the nature of the struggles regarding labor as a "field"? First, there is a struggle manifest in "Hammond's desire for omnipotence." As a slaveowner, he understood his position to be one of authority, power, and control that meant determining the meaning and nature of labor efficiency for the operation of a plantation. Second, it was assumed that slaveholders were knowledgeable (knowledge being a form of cultural and social capital) about labor management and efficiency, and that the enslaved, who actually did the work, were not. Third, objectively a slaveholder owned not only the labor of and the products produced by enslaved people, but the people themselves. Hammond interpreted that such ownership necessitated a close structuring and monitoring of enslaved people's time and lives. For Hammond, any laxity of control threatened his absolute ownership in the eyes of the enslaved and was seen as a concrete danger, decreasing his power and increasing their independence from his authority (symbolic capital). Independence could have many meanings in such a situation, ranging from the recognition of knowledge as power, to actual attempts (on the part of the enslaved) to escape to freedom. More subtly, however, independence could have meant more freedom of choice and decision-making by the enslaved. Any or all of these meanings, when recognized by enslaved persons, would diminish the omnipotence of the slaveholders.

Practice

"Practice" is activity resulting from generative schemes, perceptions, and dispositions that are fairly opaque to the actors. We have eating patterns, labor and work patterns, and religious patterns that are used, but are not conscious devices of, rational intention. Activity as "practice" is both a mode of knowledge and a way of acting which has as its basis the ordinary and everyday world, and which makes possible our experience of that world. It is multidimensional, organized and orchestrated, and outside of conscious control and discourse. Its foundation is acquired by experience of the thing or doing the thing, and in this manner, practice is "learned."

One dimension of practice is Bourdieu's notion of "dispositions." Dispositions are "interests and ways of proceeding . . . individual skills, idiosyncrasies, failings, and social competencies which are on-going learnings rooted in early childhood."[47] They are the things through which actors "know without knowing the right thing to do."[48] Incorporated into practice, dispositions are those characteristics of past learning which, in the present, are perpetuated when similarly structured situations or contexts arise.

Translated into skills learned in the doing, dispositions can become intergenerational practices. Writing about the networks of enslaved females, historian Deborah Gray White asserts:

> Skills were sometimes passed down from one generation to the next within a slave family. If a slave girl's mother was a cook, and the girl assisted her mother, then the daughter would, more than likely, assume her mother's role when the latter either was sold, grew too old, or died. Similarly, many midwives learned their skill from a female relative. The tightly guarded recipes for tonics and brews used by these "healers" were often transmitted to a younger generation by an elderly female relative.[49]

Another aspect of practice connotes a mastery or competence that is not wholly conscious or unconscious. Bourdieu says practices are embodied first and created in discourse second.[50] Practices arise from deep levels of structuring the nature of reality, a structuring which first takes place in the human body. In this sense, the body metaphorically acts as the organizing location of learning, as well as the location for generative sensation and perception—that is, as Beverly W. Harrison says, "if we begin . . . with 'our bodies, ourselves,' we recognize that all our knowledge, including our moral knowledge, is body-mediated."[51]

Such a notion has clear implications for understanding the meaning of embodiment for persons, black and white, which are inscribed by skin color-coding. In Bourdieu's terms, skin color can be seen as either cultural or symbolic capital, both in the practices of the slaveholder and the enslaved. In the opening chapter of the slave narrative *Louisa Picquet, the Octoroon,* the racially white narrator and interviewer reports:

> Louisa Picquet, the subject of the following narrative . . . was easy and graceful in her manners, of fair complexion and rosy cheeks, with dark eyes, a flowing head of hair with no perceptible inclination to curl, and every appearance, at first view, of an accomplished white lady.

No one, not appraised of the fact, would suspect that she
had a drop of African blood in her veins; indeed, few will
believe it, at first, even when told it.[52]

The interviewer has described Picquet from the standpoint of skin
color and gender inscriptions learned "not wholly consciously or
unconsciously" in the minds of white men, and has applied this to
enslaved African women who fit a certain conception of femininity. In particular, Picquet reminds the interviewer of white women
who exhibit the bodily gentility of women in the construction of
the Cult of True Womanhood.[53] Picquet's hair is described using
the notions of white women's beauty—"flowing" and with no
"inclination to curl." This is not the description of African or
African American women's natural hair texture. Picquet is further
described as being "easy and graceful in her manners" and having
the look of "an accomplished white lady."

These attributes are the prescriptions for not only femininity,
but refinement and distinction as well. As such, they are relative
forms of cultural and symbolic capital. Such inscriptions can be
used in a variety of ways depending on the agents, stakes, and
interests. One way was to make the fair-skinned colored enslaved woman an exception to the normative vulgar image of
enslaved women. Another avenue was to make the abolitionist
male interviewer and his social world more comfortable with
images of enslaved women. Yet another would be just the
opposite—that is, to unintentionally alarm his readers of the
reality of miscegenation.

Paradoxically, practiced dispositions of skin color inscription
also worked to the detriment of enslaved women. Harriet Jacobs'
narrative depicts a chilling incident in which an entire enslaved
family is brought to ruin because of the inscription of skin color,
miscegenation, and a challenge to prevailing practices of the slavocracy. An enslaved "husband" has argued with his wife publicly
enough to incur a severe whipping. Jacob writes:

There were many conjectures as to the cause of this terrible punishment. Some said . . . the slave had quarreled

with his wife in the presence of the overseer, and had accused his master of being the father of her child. They were both black, and the child was very fair.

The poor man lived, and continued to quarrel with his wife. A few months later, Dr. Flint handed them both over to a slavetrader . . . When the mother was delivered into the trader's hands, she said "You *promised* to treat me well." To which he replied, "You have let your tongue run too far; damn you!" She had forgotten that it was a crime for a slave to tell who was the father of her child.[54]

Skin color, as deeply inscribed dispositional practices of both slaveholders and the enslaved, became cultural or symbolic capital and was gained or lost in a conflict based on these arbitrarily constructed divisions. Furthermore, conflict became never-ending as intergroup conflict and competition emerged and was sustained between women and men on the basis of race.[55] The promise assumed by the enslaved woman was potentially symbolic capital that could have brought her perhaps better material conditions. Instead, it was lost in internalized divisions based on skin color and a taboo sexual liaison. As will be seen later, such an incident could also be analyzed from Scott's framework of the "hidden transcript," that in this case became public and costly.

In *Distinction*,[56] Bourdieu analyzes the embodied practices of food consumption. Taste is socially constructed and becomes part of cultural capital. In advanced capitalist France, for example, upper-class menus are defined by such foods as fine fish and delicate pastries. Such practices exemplify the ability to acquire these expensive commodities and also to inscribe symbolically those who eat such foods with the distinction of refinement. On the other hand, working-class people (particularly the men) have consumption practices of eating heavy meats and lots of starches because their choice is one of necessity as distinguished from the "freedom" of refinement.

Applying this analogy to the social relations of slavery, slaveholders or the upper class would enjoy meats, vegetables, and grains not simply as food patterns, but as economic and racial symbols of status. Enslaved women and men, however, had a consumption practice of eating starches and grains, having meats only on rare occasions, with the exception of bacon or fat pork. The following is an example: "Ration day was Saturday. Each person was given a peck of corn meal, four pounds of wheat flour, four pounds of pork meat, quart of molasses, one pound of sugar, the same of coffee and a plug of tobacco. Potatoes and vegetables came from the family garden and each slave family was required to cultivate a separate garden."[57] In the everyday eating practices of the slave plantation, the freedom of refinement displayed itself in the face of those whose food choices were ensnared by necessity. It allowed the refined to observe with moral equanimity the bodies of the enslaved, especially when these exhibited evidence of malnutrition.

This idea of the body as a site of practice, and as a metaphor for deep-structured modes of knowing, is applicable also to the religious conversion experience of the enslaved. Religious conversion, according to Riggins Earl, Jr., was a foundational experience for the African American self. The cosmology of African traditional religions provided a spirit world that allowed "the comin' of the Spirit" to be seen in the activities of daily, concrete life. People "got up" with the powerful force of the Spirit, slapping their hands, walking around in place, shouting, and seeing visions.[58] Such comings could happen in the field while at work, in a hush arbor prayer meeting, or in one's sleep. Subversive power was acquired through the embodied practices of the religion of the enslaved.

Although not always incorporated into the legal corpus of slaveholding states, the body was also a site of symbolic violence by whites. Judge John B. O'Neall of the Court of Appeals of South Carolina wrote, as part of his summary in *State vs. Harden* in 1832: "Free negroes belong to a degraded caste of society; they are in no respect on an equality with a white man. According to their condition, they ought by law to be compelled to demean themselves as inferiors, from whom submission and respect to the whites, in all their intercourse in society, is demanded."[59] The performance even of free black persons, as inscribed bodies, was to display (to whites) enslaved subservient status. This construction within the law as applied to free blacks in Augusta, Georgia, in 1843 indicates how bodily practice was socially and legally constructed for the public space. For example, "Free negroes were forbidden to ride or drive about the city save on business . . . Nor were they allowed to carry canes, clubs, or sticks, unless blind, nor smoke in public places, attend military parades, hawk beer, cake, fruit, confectionery in the streets and alleys of town, nor keep shops where the latter is sold."[60] In the everyday world of slavery—eating, walking, eye contact, voice tone and level—bodies (both black and white) were deeply encoded with meanings. Laws such as this one indicate the degree to which the bodies of both enslaved and free blacks were legally inscribed so that practices, mannerisms, and even dispositions came under the purview of white construction of the body as social space. These meanings reflected power relations controlled by whites.

Habitus

To establish the nature of everyday competencies and modes of knowing, practices and dispositions are produced and reproduced within the framework of the *habitus*. *Habitus* is Bourdieu's second major conceptual tool in the logic of practice. Bourdieu takes the term from the Latin, *habitus,* meaning a habitual or typical condition, a state or appearance, particularly of the body, and notes its appearance in the works of Hegel, Husserl, Weber, Durkheim, and Mauss.[61] Strictly speaking, Bourdieu defines *habitus* as

> the systems of durable, transposable dispositions, structured structures predisposed to function as structuring structures, i.e. as principles of the generation and structuring of practices and representations which can be objectively 'regulated' and regular without in any way being the product of obedience to rules, objectively adapted to their goals without presupposing a conscious aiming at ends or an express mastery of the operations necessary to attain them and, being all this, collectively orchestrating action of a conductor . . .[62]

Its essence is dispositions and generative principles embodied in real persons and groups, and is therefore a retention of the relationship between the body and social structures, as implied in the original Latin meaning.[63] In other words, "*habitus* is a set of dispositions evolved into practices inclining agents to act and react in certain ways."[64]

One means of understanding *habitus* is through its relational nature for both individuals and the groups to which they belong. In this sense, it functions much like the term *culture,* thereby orienting persons and groups to the social world or space. *Habitus* makes possible the internalization of objective structures of which agents are a part, and makes possible the externalization of agents' practices and dispositions—each belonging to the everyday, ordinary, and taken-for-granted world. As such, *habitus* is the outcome of the collective history of an individual and of the group. Simultaneously, it is the result and outcome of the objective structures in which individuals and groups live; it is also the history of objective relations. In this sense, *habitus* is a dialectic tool between the individual, group, and society expressing both a sense of one's place and a sense of the place of others (that is, in Weberian terms, classifications and statuses; in Marxian terms, classes).

Thus, the existence and patterns of enslaved women's work were, in part, practices of both the African and the American enslaved past, which took on "thingness" according to the specific conditions of enslavement. This complexity of *habitus* can be seen in the antebellum slave-made quilt. Gladys-Marie Frye believes that "Quilts were produced by Black women for utilitarian and decorative purposes in both White and Black households. Quilts made for Whites are hardly distinguishable from traditional Anglo-American ones. However, those quilts made for personal use of Blacks (very few examples survive) were designed and stitched in the African tradition."[65] The remarkable existence of African designs and stitching patterns exemplify African common aesthetic orientations, or in Bourdieu's parlence, "durable, transposable, structured structures." In this way, *habitus* functions in the several ways which Bourdieu's theory makes clear. Representations, which may or may not be confined by regular rules of construction and having acquired generative schemes particular to the conditions of which they are an element, image collective histories of people.

Habitus is also a "system of cognitive and motivating structures, . . . a world of already realized ends, procedures to follow, paths to take . . . and of objects endowed with permanent teleological character."[66] It is *habitus* that conditions the forms of perceptions and anticipations of the real world, whether or not those perceptions mis-recognize the arbitrariness of the constructions. Neither the external nor the internal generation of practices in the *habitus* is freestanding one from the other. This is the process (according to Bourdieu) of creating objective meaning. In the context of slavery, *habitus* is what permits general, unconscious practices, and dispositions to take on the mundane and reasonable familiarity, for both the enslaved as a group and slaveholders as a group.

Bourdieu sees *habitus* as the mirror in which people view themselves in their gender and are viewed by others; or legally view themselves and are viewed by others; or economically view themselves and are viewed by others. As such, this conceptual tool allows me to analyze chattel slavery—the social world of objective and subjective relations based on the white ownership of African and African American people—as *habitus,* which is the principle of its production and reproduction, of its order and ongoing practices.

Class and Violence

Habitus is also class *habitus.* Class is a mode of social grouping defined by a specific set of social relations. It is not simply a category of economic materialism defining everything in relation to the means of economic production (as in Marxism). Rather for Bourdieu, class is used as a universal explanatory principle for all relations. It is not real groups of people, but it is the conditioning that differentiates the existence of peoples within social spaces.

Critical for this endeavor, class and status are initially and generally the determinants of the position individuals and groups have in fields over the struggle for power. As previously demonstrated, dispositional practices in class and status social spaces generally yield regular and regulated access to and use of forms of power, primarily noted as capital. In addition to dispositional practices, class is also a category for Bourdieu which enables not only distinction in embodiment, manners, and taste; class, as a conceptual tool, also permits the investigation of hierarchical modes and uses of "symbolic power" or "symbolic violence" in the social world shared by classes—for example, slaveholders, their wives, overseers, and the enslaved. For Bourdieu, "symbolic violence" is that which is "censored, euphemized, that is, misrecognized, recognized violence . . . practical denial [of violence] which in content and action conceals the potential for real physical and overt violence."[67]

Chattel slavery was an institution that required both overt, physical violence and symbolic violence. In a graphic form, Drew Faust writes:

> [James Henry] Hammond soon regulated his white-controlled religious exercises by hiring itinerant ministers for Sunday afternoon slave services. Here the speakers undoubtedly emphasized the virtues of obedience to masters terrestrial and divine. While the whip served as the most potent symbol of physical domination, the pulpits of the Methodist and Baptist churches erected on the plantation during the 1840's became an embodiment of Hammond's crusade for ideological hegemony.[68]

Religion, being a field of contested power between specialized agents (itinerant, white-appointed ministers) and black religious leaders (enslaved or free) was also a mechanism of symbolic power and violence. Faust reports that Hammond wrote, "[I] Intend to break up negro preaching and negro churches . . . order night meetings on the plantation to be discontinued."[69] Furthermore, Hammond only permitted enslaved people to attend the church in which he held membership. It is clear that symbolic violence was required to avoid symbolic threat to his authority posed by black preachers. In this account, the dominant authority, power, and symbolic violence was understood as a means to thwart the use of physical and symbolic resistance on the part of the enslaved.

Harriet Jacobs writes of the irony of physical and symbolic violence in her chapter, "Fear of Insurrection": "Not far from this time Nate Turner's insurrection broke out; and the news threw our town into great commotion. Strange that they should be so alarmed, when their slaves were so 'contented and happy'! But so it was."[70]

In a less dramatic fashion, symbolic violence could be seen in the everyday lives of enslaved women. Jacobs recounts that after receiving a new pair of shoes from her grandmother as a child, Mrs. Flint ordered her to "Take them off, and if you put them on again, I'll throw them into the fire." Adding injury to insult, Mrs. Flint then sent Jacobs, barefoot, on a long-distance errand through the snow.[71]

Embedded in this vignette, Bourdieu's notion of cultural capital, as well as that of symbolic violence, can be clearly understood. Jacobs' shoes, a gift from the free grandmother, were material objects that many enslaved people were neither given nor permitted to wear. As such, they represented cultural capital obtained from a blackwoman with means. Flint's wife, learning that Jacobs had shoes and ones that were new, used the opportunity to turn Jacobs' cultural capital into injury and loss.

By means of threat of this symbolic violence, cultural capital was lost, and real violence ensued when Jacobs became ill as a result of walking barefoot in the snow. One can surmise that the combination of symbolic violence, loss of cultural capital, and the occasion of real violence was nearly shattering to the survival of the young Jacobs. She wrote, "That night I was very hoarse; and I went to bed thinking the next day would find me sick, perhaps dead. What was my grief on waking to find myself quite well!"[72] Although not present in Jacobs' narrative, there can be little doubt why enslaved people created such resources as the spiritual, "All God's chillun got shoes"[73] as a means of resisting the domination of slaveholders and sustaining their spirits beyond the reach of such worldly hegemony.

Pierre Bourdieu's theory of a logic of practice is capable of delineating the relationship between the objective structures of a mode of domination and the practices of individuals, groups, and classes in the social world. With the conceptual tools of field, practice, *habitus,* and class, Bourdieu would have us see agency in the social world as a combination of everyday ordinary practices and dispositions, acquired through a *habitus,* and the pursuit of power within relatively autonomous but interacting arenas comprising the social world. It is a theory that assists us in locating objective structures and human agency within history rather than in an ahistorical determinism. Finally, his theory attempts to make sense out of the more deeply structured patterns of embodiment when it is the site of dispositional practices in the struggle to dominate, and also to resist that domination.

Yet, I think Bourdieu inadequately addresses the power of subordinated individuals and groups to resist and subvert the dominant objective structures, even if they must do so in ways which appear passive, ineffective, and short term. In order to view the power of the dominated groups in structured and structuring situations, I now turn to the work of James C. Scott, political scientist.

The Resistance Art of Hidden Transcripts

In investigating the narratives of enslaved women, there exists what Scott calls "the hidden transcript . . . derivative [of the public transcript] in the sense that it consists of those offstage speeches, gestures, and practices that confirm, contradict, or inflect what appears in the public transcript."[74] The "public transcript" is a means of describing the "open interaction between subordinates and those who dominate them."[75] Scott's "broad purpose is the suggestion of a method by which one can more adequately read, interpret, and understand the often fugitive conduct of subordinate groups" in order to "study the power relations when the powerless are often obliged to adopt a strategic pose in the presence of the powerful and when the powerful may have an interest in over-dramatizing their reputation and mastery . . ."[76] It is in the slave narratives that one finds testimony to the elementary forms of domination and overt violence which affect the everyday practices and dispositions, and means of power struggles.

Utilization of Scott's notion of "hidden transcripts" must be modified in light of the slave narratives of the mature period of slavery, 1830 to 1865. The earlier discussion of the slave narrative as historical text indicated that those of the period under consideration were produced by fugitive or ex-enslaved persons often in the context of the abolitionist movements, black and white. The interviews of the WPA Slave Narrative Collection, with few exceptions, were done by white interviewers in the context of the Jim Crow South of the 1920s and '30s. Thus, the majority of narratives utilized in this study were created in the nexus precisely of the public and the hidden.

Paradoxically, the narratives serve as a public transcript or better yet, as a public declaration of refusal to submit to domination. They are "public" in the sense that they were published as narratives or interviews so that the public discourses on slavery would reflect the experience of the enslaved. In doing so, the narratives serve as a vehicle through which to see the practical success and/or failure of resistance (which may or may not have breached the normative relations of oppression), as well as a public protest which did breach the regular operations of slavery.[77]

To take seriously the view of the slave narrative and thus the practices of enslaved women as hidden transcripts adds depth to Bourdieu's theoretical model in relation to the conceptual tools of practice, disposition, and *habitus*. Hidden transcripts have three characteristics. Like practices themselves, the hidden transcript encompasses more than words of "the speech act" spoken to or about the slave master or mistress. It captures a range of practices that are inclusive of skills and competencies, like clandestine organization of the religious life, or folk medicine, or aspects of community cohesion and mutual discipline, or other forms of countersocialization in the enslaved community.

The role of the midwife or of the root woman in the life of an enslaved community was vital and serves as an example of hidden transcripts. According to Deborah Gray White, "Old bondwomen were likely to attend all slave births and all slave deaths. Their accumulated knowledge delivered one into life, helped one survive it, and sometimes, . . . hastened one to an early grave . . . as midwife and doctor they embodied the link between the generations."[78] The practices of the midwife were significant in several regards. It can be assumed that she was a source of information for healing; a source of information about family genealogies, both black and white; a source of information about events and developments in the surrounding area, gathered as she traveled; and a source of moral wisdom for the community.

The hidden transcript is also a specific social space or site of a particular group of actors. The enslaved community may be rural or town oriented, and, as a result, employ different methods or means of community building that may or may not be inclusive of free blackpersons, depending on locale. It can be representative of a social site within a given parameter, such as the hidden transcript of enslaved house servants in contrast to those who work in the fields, or those whose work is primarily that of child care, contrasted to those who are "hired out" to work for others.

The social space of hidden transcripts could be gendered spaces as well, where work was done in collective styles and rhythms. Eliza Washington reported that, "I heard mother say she went to a lot of quiltings. I suppose they had them same as they do now. Everybody took a part of the quilt to finish. They talked and sang and had a good time. And they had something to eat at the close just as they did in the corn shucking."[79] Given the nature of the workday on many plantations, women frequently had such gendered social places—the laundry, the child-care area, and where food was prepared for field hands, a common cooking area. Within such spaces, women were able to socialize girl children, discuss matters of the enslaved quarter, and give mutual aid and encouragement.

Furthermore, the hidden transcript may represent what Scott calls "a zone of constant struggle" that points to a discursive arena where public transcripts of slaveholders and the hidden transcripts of the enslaved vie for maximum or minimal control and power respectively.[80] In enslaved women's lives, one such combat zone was the kitchen in the "big house." It was often the site of disputes between slave mistress and enslaved cook, or the site of confrontation between a white child and her nurse, or between slave-owner and a group of slaves. In this sense, a hidden transcript represents a strategic discourse recording deference and survival, risk and defiance, alternative culture and rebellion—all parts of a complex way of remaining human in the face of dehumanization.

Scott's most important contributions and corrections to Bourdieu's theory of practice include his discussions of false consciousness and his rejection of the Neo-Marxist notion of ideological hegemony. He believes that the dominated have alternative ways of seeing the contradictions in the established order and have the capacity to critique them. Slave narratives reveal Scott's claim to be true. An ex-slave from Texas demonstrates Scott's claim: "Dey allus done tell us ut am wrong to lie and steal, but why did de white folks steal my mammy and her mammy?"[81] Bourdieu contends that within structure, *habitus,* and power, the functions of the established order limit alternative representations, recognition of classifications and forms of power. Thus, agents' chances of neutralizing those effects, which are most contradictory to their interests, can be done only through compliance with those very dimensions in order to use them to their own ends.

The implication of Bourdieu's view is not only that change occurs within the specific field, but more important, there appears to be an underlying skepticism that is twofold. Conscious intention is, in itself, inadequate as a motivating factor because of the deep inscription of the mis-recognition and its naturalization. Moreover, he claims that the dominated, although needing to use the resources and regularities of the established order, also make a virtue of necessity: "The objective limits [of the social world] become a sense of limits, a practical anticipation of objective limits acquired by experience of objective limits, a 'sense of one's place' which leads one to exclude oneself from the goods, persons, places, and so forth from which one is excluded."[82]

Scott challenges this assumption by suggesting that practical anticipation of objectives may be something that can be attributed to both the elite and the subordinate. However, he argues against the degree to which Bourdieu can claim full ideological incorporation of the subculture of dominated groups into that of the dominant groups. Hidden transcripts for Scott demonstrate hidden grievances, alternative social organization, and other practices that are assumed to be repressed by the hegemony of the dominant. His point is that the supposed ideological incorporation of the subordinated neither validates the lack of social conflict present in arenas of domination, nor assumes that subordinates believe that their situation is inevitable.[83] Recalling that most of the enslaved were prohibited from learning to read and write, and therefore kept "unknowledgeable," ex-enslaved woman Susan Rhodes comments, "People in my day didn't know book learning but dey studied how to protect each other, and save 'em from much misery and grieve."[84]

In fact, Scott believes that, if there is acceptance of the dominant ideology or symbolic capital on the part of subordinates, it can often increase the probability of conflict, since the inherent contradictions in the ideology become visible to them. Returning to Bourdieu's aversion to a role of conscious intention, Scott adheres to an understanding of the rich depth of alternative visions—"the fantasy life"—of subordinated groups. He argues against absolutizing hegemony, even though objective structures make elements such as upward mobility or overt rebellion and victory outside ordinary and everyday expectations seem doubtful. Scott offers instead a reading of hidden transcripts, which depicts a notion of the "popular imagination"[85] of the dominated. First, Scott defends popular imagination by asserting that the serf or slave can imagine a total reversal of the established order where power, wealth, status, and material goods are in their hands. Not only have such visions been imagined, they have been inscribed as well in practices, folktales, songs, and rituals of the subordinated.

One type of "popular imagination" can be found in the folktales of enslaved men and women. Ranging in their themes, the nature of their characters, and the purpose of the story and storyteller, folktales provided the enslaved with a means to dream justice, seek revenge, express protest, and more. One such folktale about revenge went as follows: "[A slave] wen' to a witch man.

When his master 'mence to whip him, eve'y cut he give de man, his [master's] wife way off at home feel de cut. Sen' wor' please stop cut lick de man. When he [master] got home, his wife was wash down wid blood."[86] Stories such as these also serve to disempower the violence and slave master, and to channel in more positive and self-affirming directions the powerlessness enslaved people often felt in the face of abuse.

Historian Lawrence Levine notes how the Hebrew Bible was used in an ideological and utopian fashion in slave religion. Indicating the overlap between songs, sermons, and other fragments that fostered the "promulgation of stability" and that fostered "discontent," Levine writes that "the similarity of the [Hebrew Bible] tales to the situation of the slaves was too clear for them not to see it; too clear for us to believe that the songs had no worldly content for blacks in bondage."[87] He cites the slave spiritual, "O My Lord Delivered Daniel," in which the enslaved sang, "He delivered Daniel from de lion's den, Jonah from de belly ob de whale, And de Hebrew children from de fiery furnace, And why not every man?"[88]

Second, Scott submits that the dominated have been able to envision more equitable societies in which there is the absence of distinctions used to stratify power relations. He understands this ability in the subordinated as the ability to negate the existing social order.[89] No greater resource than religion provides continual examples of alternative vision and negation of the existing social order. In Protestant Christianity, the biblical testimony abounded in such stories as the Exodus—the Promised Land tradition, the parables of the Laborers in the Vineyard, or Lazarus and the Rich Man, and in stories such as Annanias and Sapphira.[90] As utopian thought, according to Scott, religious language and use of sacred scripture could disguise belief or expectations considered revolutionary. In addition, such thinking also provided a critical set of mobilizing ideas for actual rebellion. Cases in point are the Denmark Vesey and Nat Turner slave insurrections in which religious language imaged the final blood judgment from God.[91]

These last citations also attest to Scott's argument that both the reversal and negation of the social order by the dominated indicate that such groups have, in fact, acted upon the values and beliefs embedded in them. On the modest end of the spectrum, Scott believes that such beliefs enabled daily sabotage, subversion, and protection against the internalization of dehumanization. At the extreme end, they fueled uprisings (even when there was more hope than the situation realistically suggested).

For my purposes, James Scott's analysis and refinement of Bourdieu's theory opens up a different reading on the social space and aspirations of the oppressed through his notion of hidden transcripts. This notion is open to seeing, as Bourdieu does, the power of the established order to control and define life. Yet, it also offers possibilities of viewing the strategies of the enslaved not simply as reactions to domination, but as building social spaces relatively free from, and alternative to, life under domination.

In the next chapter, I analyze as a womanist the lived experience of enslaved African American women in these structures. While elements of Bourdieu's and Scott's framework assist in the locating and connecting of the objective and social-relational aspects of the social world of enslavement, the overarching framework will be the womanist ethical framework approaching blackwomen's moral agency in the struggle for emancipation and self-determined quality of life. Critique and reflection upon this relationship will provide the view and meaning of enslaved African American women as moral agents in relation to their work in slavery and their work for emancipation.

3

By Perseverance and Unwearied Industry

> To speak of a work ethic is not to ask how much work a
> people did, or even how much work they thought they
> should do, although the latter is getting tolerably close. It
> is to ask of a people what meaning did work have in their
> own conceptualization of their social existence. In this
> sense, the work ethic of a people is so securely bound to
> their collective *Weltanschauung* as to make meaningless
> any attempt to transcend a given collective experience.
> Thus the alteration of social relations embedded in
> slavery would precipitate a change in the very meaning
> of the concept of work itself.[1]

Jaynes' words rang true in my mind and crystallized my interest in the meaning of work, in African American historic
existence, and our worldview. Those words have supported my
intuition that work was not and is not an individualistic endeavor.
Work and labor are measured by self, familial, and community
survival and nurture rather than by individual economic success
or other values of the dominant society—values that oppress
rather than liberate communities of blackpeople. I want to discover the collective origins of African American Christians' work
ethic, or at least theorize about it. In particular, I want to understand the development of such an ethic as it was grounded in the
lives of blackwomen.

Religion is one dimension of life which shapes the *Weltan-schauung* of a people, and which often gives meaning to other cultural conceptualizations of life. To use Bourdieu's construct, it is the "religious field" in a people's social world. From the beginning of North American British colonization, and later during U.S. independence, religion was a primary force in shaping the social order of the New World. It stood side by side with chattel slavery and defined the external world of the enslaved as a world of work, production, and lifelong ownership by and for others. This New World religion, and especially Protestantism, was desperately needed "in order to create the moral rigor and social solidarity guarantee[ing] the survival of the fragile community."[2] This is especially so in the sense that religion functions to legitimize the dominant (or in this case, the emerging social order). The Church believed its primary mission was the conversion of all New World peoples—Indians, Africans, and Europeans—to the Gospel, and secondarily, the establishment of an ordered society which could accomplish community cohesion. This, according to Donald G. Mathews, was particularly true of the southern colonies prior to the American Revolution, and on through the great southern migration of 1812.[3]

In the context of southern slaveholding from the seventeenth century onward, Protestantism developed several views concerning what ought to be "the appropriate relation of the human to the divine and of the legitimate relations among people . . . [This view] ultimately led to a commitment to slavery as a necessary social [as well as economic] system and to a defense of slavery as the best possible bulwark against the corrosive and un-Christian impact" of developing northern industrial capitalism and its social relations.[4] Put simplistically yet accurately, proslavery evangelical Protestantism came to hold the view that the soul of the enslaved belonged to God but that the body and labor of the enslaved belonged to his or her owner. Moreover,

> it emphasized the moral responsibilities of both masters and slaves . . . [and argued that Christian faith] provided

blacks with the external restraint necessary to curb their licentiousness and emotionalism on the one hand, and . . . a cultural apprenticeship in family life, self-discipline, responsibility, and Christian commitment.[5]

From the perspective of white masters, religion defined their responsibility as Christian slaveholders and offered their slaves righteousness—or the raising of moral standards. In the words of a white missionary to slaves, "The Gospel . . . teaches [the Negro] obedience to God, and faithfulness to the interests of his earthly master."[6] To this we can add that the slaveholding society believed that Christian faith instilled notions of obedience and vocation. The Methodist slave catechism put it this way:

> Question: What is the meaning of "Thou shall not commit adultery"?
> Answer: To serve our heavenly Father, and our earthly master, obey our overseer, and not steal anything.
> Question: What did God make you for?
> Answer: To make a crop.[7]

The development of proslavery Protestant views, then, exemplify the external economic, social, and religious dimensions of slave status and indoctrination in the interrelated fields of work and religion. Coupled with the slaveholders' demands for efficiency and maximum productivity, these views combined to create the slaveholders' notion of a work ethic for the enslaved: Slaves, obey your masters. However, it does not reveal the internal and communal understanding the enslaved themselves had about their own situation, particularly their understanding of God and of work beyond the context of the chattel relationship. Slave historiographers, theologians, and ethicists have often debated the existence of a slave work ethic. They use planter journals, preachers' sermons, and male slave narratives.[8] Yet none have explored this issue from the perspective of enslaved African American women, and none through an investigation of enslaved women's narratives.

A womanist exploration into a constructive work ethic of enslaved antebellum women (in female slave narratives) initially locates four characteristics of such an ethic:

1. blackwomen's theological and ethical understanding of the relation of God to slavery;

2. womanish moral authority, instruction, and action as an intergenerational dynamic for communal maintenance, empowerment, and solidarity in the context of oppression (inclusive of occasional crossings of racial boundaries);

3. blackwomen's struggle for self-determination in the use of one's own sexual and reproductive labor; and

4. blackwomen's work-related attitudes of self-reliance, and confidence in one's own learned craft and skill.

I define a "work ethic" as a motivating vision of livelihood—that is, the creation and use of intuition, skills, and practices which allow for the sustaining of self and family, and which contribute to the process of liberation from oppression for one's community of accountability. Together, these four characteristics suggest that the nature and meaning of work itself is found in the quest for concrete freedom and human wholeness in the face of humanly constructed oppression and evil.

My task for this chapter is the investigation of blackwomen's self-understanding of work *unchained* from slavery's meaning, yet *arising out of those very chains.* In what follows, I will use womanist sensibilities to understand blackwomen's struggle to subvert and liberate themselves and their community from these chains. I will also employ the theories of Pierre Bourdieu and James C. Scott to remind the reader of the interplay of the logic of practice structuring those chains.

Enslaved Women's Faith in the God of Freedom

In the Works Progress Administration (WPA) Slave Narrative Collection, the ex-slaves' testimony clearly demonstrates that slaves did not believe that slavery was the will of God.[9] Sarah Ford told a WPA interviewer, "Lawd me, de heaps of things go on in slave times what won't go on no more, 'cause de bright light come and it ain't dark no more for us black folks." Ford goes on to recall how Old Uncle Lew was preaching one day about how the Lord made everyone "in unity on one level"; the next day, the slave master heard about it, and put Old Uncle Lew out in the field with the rest of the slaves.[10] The imagery of "bright light" contrasted to the "dark" may sound like internalized racist language to this generation of blackpeople. However, it unmistakably refers to the Good News that enslaved women (and men) had in God, especially in the midst of the evil of slavery, which could punish a person for preaching a theology other than the slave master's theology.

The female narratives of the mature antebellum period likewise understand that the peculiar institution was a peculiar *human* institution, not one divinely sanctioned. In fact, in the midst of the degradation that enslaved peoples experienced, many knew and attested to the fact that only God and other members of the enslaved community turned a sympathetic ear to their troubles. Old Elizabeth, born in 1766, wrote that at the time of separation and sale from her mother as a young girl, "I had none in the world to look to but God, [so] I betook myself to prayer, and in every lonely place I found an alter."[11] In the life of an enslaved woman, separated from one's kin and slave community, the world was a hostile place. It was a world of slave and slave master. In such a context of isolation, it becomes clear to enslaved women that God was different from, and not associated with, the cruelty and perversion of chattel slavery.

Similarly, yet more stoically, Elizabeth Kleckley, thirty years a slave and four years an employee in the White House, critiqued the God-understanding in the writing of those who were responsible for constitutionally legitimating slavery, saying, ". . . the God of nature and the fathers who framed the Constitution for the United States" and "the law [which] descended to [the fathers] was natural and it was natural that they should recognize it, since it was in their interest to do so."[12] Could it be that in so thinking

and writing, Kleckley drew a distinction between the impersonal
God and the deism of the founding fathers—a God who could be
seen to be distant from the workings of humans—and that of a
personally revelatory God? She continues: "God rules the Universe . . . and through me and the enslaved millions of my race,
one of the problems [slavery] was solved that belonged to the
great problem of human destiny."[13] Enslaved Sarah Ford and Old
Uncle Lew probably led lives very similar to that of most enslaved
persons—they were field hands. Kleckley's life would take her
among the most elite white political leaders, North and South.
One enslaved woman expressed her faith in the simple language
of the "invisible institution," while the other could speak of her
faith in words alluding to the nation's founding fathers and their
documents. At each end of the spectrum of enslaved life and social
status, both women firmly believed that freedom was the will of
God.

Another dimension of this moral reasoning mediates an understanding of God as a God of freedom and not of slavery, while at
the same time mediating a logic that recognizes African traditional
religious sensibilities and the larger struggle of the black community to shape its own culture. The narrative of Sojourner Truth
(known while enslaved as Isabella Bomefree) integrates these two
streams of moral reasoning. It is Mau-Mau Bett, Isabella's
mother, who teaches the slave girl about the protection of God and
God's power, as well as respect for the stars and the moon.[14] It is
her parents who share with her and her brother the memories of
her siblings who were sold or who had died, placing their lives
and her own in the continuing web of the African ancestors and
cosmos. From a later terse incident in Truth's narrative comes this
deep expression of God's power to overcome the adversities of
slavery:

> I tell you. I stretched up, and felt as tall as the world.
> "Missus," says I, "I'll have my son back again!" She
> laughed. "You will, you nigger? How you goin' to do it?
> You ha'nt got no money." No Missus but God has
> enough, or what's better! And I'll have my child again.[15]

For enslaved woman Harriet Jacobs, renewal of faith and of ancestral ties is poignantly depicted in her narrative, *Incidents in the Life of a Slave Girl*. As Jacobs prepares herself for her final escape, she returns to the graves of her mother and father:

> My spirit was overawed by the solemnity of the scene. For more than ten years I had frequented this spot, but never had it seemed to me so sacred as now . . . I knelt down and kissed them, and poured forth a prayer to God for guidance and support in the perilous step I was about to take. As I passed the wreck of the old meeting house, where before Nat Turner's Time, the slaves had been allowed to meet for worship, I seemed to hear my father's voice coming from it, bidding me not to tarry till I reached freedom or the grave. I rushed on with renovated hopes. My trust in God had been strengthened by that prayer among the graves.[16]

This is the cultural site of empowerment and the religious site of ritual (empowering) prayer to God, bringing together enslaved ancestors and the Christian God, in which strength and guidance are sought. Sterling Stuckey has reminded us that such sites are spirit-filled, conjuring, libational, or mediating spaces of empowerment between the living and the dead.[17] In the situation of enslavement, they are subversive sites of counter-religious and theological liberation.

It is important to note that not in every enslaved situation could women have such firm faith. In some cases, this was due to isolation, illiteracy, and the slave master's control. Jenny Proctor, an Alabama-born ex-enslaved woman, recounted:

> Dey wasn't no church for de slaves but we goes to white folks arbor on Sunday evenin' and a white man he gits up der to preach to the niggers. He say, 'Now I takes my text, which is, "nigger obey your marster and your mistress, 'cause what you get from dem in here in dis world am all you ev'r goin' to git, 'cause you jes' like de hogs and de other animals, when you dies you ain't no more, after you been thrown in dat hole." ' I guess we believed

dat for a while 'cause we didn't have no way findin' out
different. We didn't see no Bibles.[18]

In other cases, it was not a matter of faith. Enslaved people like
Jenny who wanted religion had to also attend the white church or
prayer meeting. Other times, it was also a matter of class or social
status on the plantation. Rebecca Grant reported, "Didn't have no
colored churches. De drivers and de overseers, de house-servants,
de bricklayers and folk like dat'd go to white folks church. But not
the field hands. Why dey couldn't have all got in de church."[19] We
can surmise, however, that enslaved folks exercised a hermeneutic
of suspicion when attending the churches of slave masters and
recognized the dissonance between their experience of slavery
and the master's religious ideology.

In each of these examples are demonstrations of the degree to
which enslaved women exhibit theological praxis—action and
reflection. From a womanist framework, these women are
engaged in discernment of theological doctrines and spiritual
understandings that uphold or liberate structures of oppression.
Sarah Ford realizes that Uncle Lew being sent to work in the fields
is a direct punishment for preaching an alternative gospel, one that
addressed the basic unity and equality of all people. This articulation directly flew in the face of the slave master as the legitimizer
of religious authority on the plantation, and of the public religious
transcript concerning the divinely sanctioned relationship
between master and slave. And it yields a very direct commentary
on enslaved women's ability to see and recognize the fine line
between symbolic violence (loss of Lew's preacher status) and the
direct, physical violence of field work under slavery.

Furthermore, these enslaved women's narratives give evidence
to the battle between the public religious transcripts and cultural
capital of the dominant culture and those of enslaved women.
Both Kleckley and Truth deconstruct the religious ideology of the
founding fathers and a slave mistress respectively, offering coun-
terinterpretations of the nature of God and of their faith in that
God. Likewise in postbellum reflection, enslaved women could
also recognize and articulate the struggle for their religious sensibilities between the opportunity to worship in an enslaved-

controlled environment and the limitations of white church attendance, or the lack of any church attendance.

Perhaps most striking is the theological praxis of enslaved
women to preserve "right" knowledge of God and "right" ritualis-
tic, communalistic reverence for the wisdom of ancestors, and
"right" moral action as a result of attention to such relationships.
Both Mau-Mau Bett and Harriet Jacobs return to a deep synthesis
of enslaved Christian faith and African traditional spirituality for
right moral action. In the former, right moral action occurs in a
moment of inspirational teaching and devotional guidance. In the
latter, right moral action proceeds spiritual strengthening for
demands of escape from enslavement. Both exemplify how theological praxis can encompass the realization of emancipatory historiography. In this way, theological praxis embodies the
reclaiming and using of a different religious memory, structure,
and logic.

From these sketches, we can assume that blackwomen's moral
reasoning was richly textured in its perception of the nature of
God and of God's relation to slavery. God was for these women:
1. sheltering; 2. in control of the universe despite the exercise of
oppression by humanity expressing its free will; and 3. fluid
enough to be both African traditional and African American Christian Redeemer of the oppressed, with resources beyond those
defined as power resources by humans. What becomes absolutely
definitive in these witnesses is a shared collective hope—
freedom—which could be voiced only rarely as a public desire,
but which needed to remain an often articulated prayer as well as
historical possibility.

Womanist Moral Authority and Instruction

The second characteristic of an enslaved women's ethics is the
witness to womanish moral authority in the instruction of
enslaved mothers, grandmothers, sisters and aunts, fathers, brothers and uncles, and the extended adopted kin-network of the slave
community. It was within this kin-network that enslaved women
learned the value and meaning of work as different from and an
alternative to the value and meaning of work experienced at the

hands of the slaveholding society. One dimension of this moral instruction manifested itself in intergenerational practices. A young enslaved female might have learned everything she knew from her mother: sewing, sock mending, cooking, and survival wisdom.

Delia Hill was quite forceful in relating the intensity with which her mother imparted moral instruction. As a child, she heard the usual injunctions from the white preacher warning slaves not to steal from their owners, and if they knew someone else who had committed theft it was the enslaved child's duty to report it. Hill indicated what her mother thought about all that by saying, "We believe dat den. We didn't know no better, honest we didn't . . . But bless your soul, our mammy done smoked 'nough of us up side down, not to tell dem white folks nothin', a lie, nor truth. No sir'ee."[20]

This moral instruction is of a twofold moral nature: It addresses moral *being* and moral *agency*. At one level it can be understood as a mother's injunction, "Don't be a liar." That would fulfill part of the obligation requested of the dominant moral injunction. On another level it can be perceived to mean, "Don't be, say, or do anything to white folks regarding this matter" (and perhaps other matters). In the second instance, the admonition has the intent of directly superseding the authority and rule of the slaveowner so that the child acts in a subversive manner to protect herself, her family and the enslaved community.

This kind of moral instruction was teaching resistance in a number of ways. Not only was a mother indirectly challenging the slave master, but she was giving lessons in individual and communal survival, since an enslaved person's indiscretion could bring disastrous results—a whipping or other punishment, or loss of any relative privilege, or even sale. In the face of such possibilities, a child needed to understand the consequences that could befall and therefore affect the entire enslaved quarter. Furthermore, a lesson about the reciprocity of production to producer was tacit in the admonition. There was no acknowledgment on the part of the mother that the taking of a hog was "stealing" the slaveowner's property. It is plausible that she was teaching a lesson about reciprocating obligations in work that rendered hogs and other property of the owner the property of enslaved people as well. In effect, the work of enslaved people provided the resources by which a slaveowner could afford a hog.

Enslaved woman Sally Williams recalls that her mother, known as Katy to everyone, taught her children the "habits of industry and activity." Sally puts it this way: "I tell you how my mother done me—she whipped me when I didn't work to please her, but 'twas the glorious thing!"[21] It seems that Sally places emphasis not on the lessons of industry taught as rules of the slaveholder, but rather on the fact that they were lessons taught by her mother. One could claim that because slaveholders impressed these lessons upon their chattel, Aunt Katy was simply reproducing the socialization of the system. A more reasonable claim can be made, however, for Aunt Katy teaching Sally that as her daughter, these things were expected of Sally. Moreover, this injunction could also contain clues for avoiding the more precarious cruelties of slave work life—whippings and beatings for work performed poorly. In either case, however, Sally's response to her mother's moral instruction and authority was: "but 'twas the glorious thing!"

Several passages from *Incidents in the Life of a Slave Girl* directly display the relationship between work and the moral authority of the kin-network. Speaking about her mother, Jacobs says, "My mother was a slave in name only, but in nature was noble and womanly."[22] To Jacobs, the title *slave* was a legal title in an unjust, oppressive social and economic system. By juxtaposing *slave* with *noble and womanly,* Jacobs attests to a more authentically true, human, and moral status for her mother, and for all enslaved mothers. Again these elements must be seen in contrast to the moral character of slaveholders (and their demand for obedience). As a child, Jacobs recalls that, "It was her [grandmother's, that is, Aunt Marthy's] labor that supplied my scanty clothes, and by perseverance and unwearied industry, a snug little home surrounded with all the necessities of life."[23] Jacobs recognized that these were moral qualities. Later, while as a fugitive slave hiding for seven years in a false floor in her grandmother's home, Jacobs retells that, "The good grandmother gave me herb tea and cooling medicines, and finally I got ridden of the [little red insects, fine as a needle's point] . . . which produced an intolerable burning."[24]

Jacobs makes two important and related moral assertions. The first is that true labor or work provides for the basic needs of persons no matter the cost. It was her father, and later her grandmother, who consistently provided her with food, clothing, shelter, and ultimately, sanctuary. Dr. Flint, her white owner, professed to care and provide comfort, and he often spoke of this to Jacobs. But he did nothing of the sort. Instead (for years before her escape), he sexually hounded Jacobs.

The second claim Jacobs makes is that the grandmother is the exemplar of moral good. She is morally good in two ways. She uses her power to heal, comfort, and listen, not only to Jacobs but also to many in their Edenton, North Carolina, town. Writing about her grandmother's plight on the auction block at the hands of Dr. Flint several years earlier, Jacobs writes:

> "Aunt Marthy," as she was called, was generally known, and everybody who knew her respected her intelligence and good character. Her long and faithful service in the family was also well known, and the intentions of her mistress [Dr. Flint's mother-in-law] to leave her free . . . When the day came for her sale, she took her place among the chattels, and at the first call she sprang upon the auction block. Many voices called out, "Shame! Shame! Who is going to sell you, aunt Marthy? Don't stand there! That is no place for *you*." No one bid for her. At last a feeble voice said, "Fifty dollars." . . . she [the sister of my grandmother's deceased mistress] was resolved to protect her . . . The auctioneer waited for a high bid; but her wishes were respected; no one bid above her . . . She gave the old servant her freedom.[25]

Aunt Marthy acts on Jacobs' behalf numerous times. On one such occasion, she has clandestinely shared Jacobs' travail within a formidable network of allies. Aunt Marthy's action brings interesting results for Jacobs, who writes:

> Among others, it chanced that a white unmarried gentle-
> man [Mr. Sands] had obtained some knowledge of the
> circumstances in which I was placed. He knew my grand-
> mother, and often spoke to me in the street. He became
> interested for me, and asked questions about my master,
> which I answered in part. He expressed a great deal of
> sympathy, and a wish to aid me.[26]

As a consequence of Aunt Marthy's actions, Jacobs becomes
involved with Sands (a white man), who would later be strategic
in obtaining freedom for Jacobs' children. Moral goodness again
is done contrary to, and in conflict with, the prevailing social
mores. Thus, the grandmother uses her power and resources for
freedom-pursuing movement, despite her very real fears in har-
boring Harriet as a fugitive slave.

Another dimension of womanish moral authority is the
bonding and solidarity between enslaved women and among
enslaved women and their allies. In Jacobs' narrative in particular,
one gets an in-depth and prolonged look at the myriad ways in
which enslaved women and their allies maneuver the social relations of slavery for the good of the enslaved community. At one
level, this bonding is attempted through the public transcript of
the narrative itself. Jacobs' goal in writing is to move more than
the moral sentiments of northern, middle-class white women
readers. She writes to express the conditions in which she and
more than two million enslaved women live. She writes to put
northern middle-class white women's lives in perspective, underlining their own freedom (in spite of their patriarchal bondage) in
relation to the bondage of Jacobs' enslaved sisters. Her intent is to
move them to action on behalf of enslaved women throughout
the South—to undermine the power, control, and authority of
slavery.

At another level, woman-bonding is done across the barriers of
class and race in Jacobs' life. Prior to an underground railroad,
there existed for many women an underground network of subversion and resistance. Into this network will be drawn not only the
lawyer Sands, but a slaveholding woman and her enslaved housekeeper, Betty.[27] It will also include Jacobs' immediate family of

aunts, uncles, and cousins; later a ship's captain as well as Philadelphia, New York, and Boston abolitionists. This network is set in an opposing position to the many formal, legal resources which the Flint family have at their disposal to prevent Jacobs' flight to freedom—bounty hunters, slave traders, and state and federal laws (for example, the Fugitive Slave Act, 1850).

Womanish moral authority and instruction emerges from the analysis of enslaved women's attempt to embody moral being and action. Within the context of the kin-network and enslaved community, an ever-evolving cycle of discernment of norms and values exists that is appropriate to the survival and enhancement of a dignified quality of life for individuals and the community. Enslaved women teach younger enslaved women to "read" the public and hidden transcripts (injunctions of slaveowners and peer pressure from other enslaved youngsters about stealing, for example) and determine the nature of the social world with their own eyes. By instructing her daughter in the expectations of work-related behavior, Sally Williams' mother, Katy, is simultaneously delegitimating the mis-recognition of the meaning of work and offering an alternative meaning having to do with the quality of the mother/daughter enslaved relationship. From the actions of Aunty Marthy, Jacobs learns to recognize the nature of moral goodness; from the actions of Dr. Flint, she learns the immorality of abuse of power. This is teaching an integrated way of being and action that is conscientization and resistance.

Enslaved women's moral authority and teaching is further illuminated as providing strategic options for action on behalf of self and community. The woman-bonding, community, and solidarity between and across racial lines in the social world of slavery, noted above, provides a clue as to how enslaved women created real and potential alternative social worlds despite the overarching objective structure of slavery. By doing so, enslaved women act to change the social world itself, even if done in small but resistant and liberating ways—that is, in the face of slaveholders' power to thwart enslaved women's attempted escapes, enslaved women create their own resources to break their bondage. Moreover, such actions continue "to keep hope alive" and offer models for other enslaved women. Seen as "hidden transcripts," these models are passed on especially through the sharing of moral authority and instruction.

Enslaved Women's Embodied Labor

The nature of moral goodness, and its relation to enslaved women's work, is the underlying theme for the third characterization of a blackwomen's work ethic. Here, blackwomen's control of their own bodies, sexuality, and reproductive capacities make a work ethic a complex matter, fraught with ambiguity. Embodiment itself becomes a matter of multiple fields of struggle in that enslaved women's bodies were multiple sites of practices, dispositions, and meanings. Enslaved women were exploited for their labor in the fields, their labor in the slaveowner's house for his/her family, and in the slave quarter, ironically performing tasks that sustained the slave master's workforce—housekeeping, cooking, sewing, and providing medical assistance. They were also exploited as sexual objects, and as breeders of the slaveowner's human capital. According to Joanne Braxton, enslaved women knew that they were "sexual" laborers and producers of children for the slave market, and that these factors made women a commodity different and unique from men.[28] And enslaved men were aware of this particularity in enslaved women's lives:

> Marse Sam never have so pow'ful many slaves. Seem lak dere was more women and chillun than men. In them days, pa tells me, a white man raise niggers just lak a man raises horse or cows. Have a whole lot of mares and 'pendin' on other man to have de stallion. Fust thing you know dere would be a whole lot of colts kickin' up their heels on de place. Lak is a white man start out wid a few women folk slaves, soon him have a plantation full of little niggers runnin' 'round un deir shirt-tails and a kickin' up deir heels, whilst deir mammies hoeing and geeing at de plow handles, workin' lak a man.[29]

In essence, the physical and emotional invasion of their bodies was intimately coercive,[30] creating a deep moral contradiction in

the lives of many enslaved women. Often, this moral struggle is
only alluded to in the narratives of enslaved women. One simple
reference (a partial hidden transcript) comes from an ex-enslaved
woman from South Carolina. When interviewed, she said, "And
dere wasn't no purity for de young girls in de slave quarters,
'cause de overseer was always sending for de young negro girls to
be with 'em, and some girl was always findin' a baby for him.
'Course, I wasn't suppose to know nothin' 'bout anything like
dis', but I hears older folks talk . . ."[31]

Elizabeth Kleckley writes of her "deep mortification during
[her] residence at Hillsboro," in only a few sentences, recalling:

> I was regarded as fair-looking for one of my race, and for
> four years a white man—I spare the world his name—
> had base designs upon me. I do not care to dwell upon
> this subject, for it is one that is fraught with pain. Suffice
> it to say, that he persecuted me for four years, and I—I
> became a mother.[32]

The subject of Kleckley's sexual persecution and exploitation is
one that is painful to her because the violation was a multiple one.
First, it reflects slaveholding society's color consciousness and
male preference for "fair-looking" blackwomen, a consciousness
clearly internalized by Kleckley. Although the reader does not
know whether Kleckley personally agrees with the dominant
society's valuation, we can assume she understood it as racially
oppressive. Other "fair-looking" enslaved women (known as
mulattos), such as Louisa Picquet, had expressed similar sentiments.[33]

Second, Kleckley's pain is the result of motherhood outside the
boundary of matrimony. She states:

> . . . If my poor boy ever suffered any humiliating pangs
> on account of his birth, he could not blame his mother, for
> God knows that she did not wish to give him life; he must
> blame the edicts of that society which deemed it no crime
> to undermine the virtue of girls in my then position.[34]

The fear of her child facing future humiliation is central to the second half of the passage. The reader learns that, because of this pain—present and future—this child "was the only child that I ever brought into this world."[35] Readers of enslaved women's narratives know that often such fear for the humiliation of their white-fathered children was real. Jacobs' reunion with her daughter provides an excellent example, when her daughter Ellen recalls the treatment she received from Mr. Sands, her white father:

> I know all about it . . . I am nothing to my father, and he is nothing to me . . . I was with him five months in Washington, and he never cared for me. He never spoke to me as he did to his little Fanny. I knew all the time he was my father, for Fanny's nurse told me so; but she said I must never tell anybody, and I never did. I used to wish that he would take me in his arms and kiss me, as he did Fanny; or that he would sometimes smile at me, as he did at her. I was a little girl then, and didn't know any better.[36]

Further, Louisa Picquet makes abundantly clear her own sense of futility about skin color and her white-fathered children in her interview with Hiram Mattison. In responding to Mattison's question regarding the mulatto color of her children, Picquet states, "No, Sir! They were all white. They look just like him. After a while he got so disagreeable that I told him, one day, I wished he would sell me, or 'put me in his pocket'. . . because I had no peace at all. I rather die than live in that way."[37]

Third, Kleckley's claim to be blameless, and her invocation of God's knowledge and understanding of her situation, indicates Kleckley's sense of her moral position and of her innocence in the face of violation. This passage is descriptive of Kleckley's feelings, and those feelings and violations experienced by slave women in general. Moreover, it is an address to her audience as justification of her moral standards in an unjust society. In doing so, Kleckley intimates the nature of the double standard by which the lives and work of enslaved women are judged—the cult of true womanhood. Social conventions characterizing the ideal woman between the 1820s and the Civil War emphasized piety, purity, submissiveness, and domesticity as the path to fulfillment for women. It was the social standard by which white women understood their role and place in patriarchal southern society. And it was the moral, political, and economic yardstick by which enslaved women were excluded from the definition of woman. Hazel Carby writes:

> As a slave, the black woman was in an entirely different relation to the plantation patriarch [than was the white slave mistress]. Her reproductive destiny was bound to capital accumulation; black women gave birth to property and, directly, to capital itself in the form of slaves, and all slaves inherited their status from their mothers.[38]

In addition, Carby writes:

> A basic assumption of the principles underlying the cult of true womanhood was the necessity for the white female to "civilize" the baser instincts of man. But in the face of what was constructed as the overt sexuality of the black female, excluded as she was from the parameters of virtuous possibilities, these baser male instincts were entirely uncontrolled.[39]

Harriet Jacobs' *Incidents* most comprehensively addresses enslaved women's moral self-understanding in the face of the cult of true womanhood. Jacobs' manner of introducing the fact of her affair with an unmarried white lawyer (a strategy for repelling the sexual pursuit of her owner and relatively taking her sexuality into her own hands) begins with the statement, ". . . but the condition of a slave confuses all the principles of morality, and in fact, renders the practice of them impossible."[40] Furthermore, she writes, "When they told me my new-born babe was a girl, my heart was heavier than it had ever been."[41] Jacobs knew that enslaved girls and women faced wrongs, sufferings, and mortification peculiarly their own. Thus, women like Kleckley, Picquet, and Jacobs inescapably understood that enslavement entailed the prospects of sexual labor as well as reproductive labor.

An aspect of labor critical to this discussion is the work-related role of the mammy because it bridges the reality of enslaved women's embodied labor and their everyday work and moral agency—my third and fourth characteristics of an enslaved women's work ethic. Historiographically, Catherine Clinton claims that the mammy image—blackwomen who ran white households and served as the "right hand" of plantation mistresses—was an actuality only in a handful of cases during the fifty years following the Revolutionary War.[42] Deborah Gray White asserts that, "most of what we know about Mammy comes from memoirs written after the Civil War."[43] Both historians agree that the mammy figure is a representation created by white Southerners to favorably characterize the relationship between whites and blacks in its slave society, and negatively portray the black family and black female sexuality. Therefore, it is important to recognize that the image of the "aunty" or mammy is steeped in a multifaceted conceptualization of white, racial constructions.

White's historiographical research provides the data from postbellum memoirs of white women that create a composite of this constructed woman. The mammy is the enslaved woman who:

- could do anything, and do it better than anyone else;
- made all other household servants her subordinates;
- was reliable and trustworthy—ruled with a "rod of iron";
- was the general superintendent of all the younger servants and was a cook who ruled supreme in the kitchen;
- gave out work and taught the plantation women to sew;
- managed the whole big and mixed household;
- was the one called upon when anything was required, day or night; and
- had privileges and influence (if not power) in relation to the plantation master and mistress.

White ends her composite sketch by stating, "She was the house servant who was given complete charge of domestic management. She served also as friend and advisor. She was, in short, surrogate mistress and mother."[44]

More specifically, Harriet Jacobs' narrative gives us a view of the aunty or mammy from the perspective of an enslaved family member, albeit one with relative cultural and symbolic capital. Jacobs' great-aunt, Aunt Nancy (her mother's twin sister), was a slave in the Flint household, and was described as "the *factotum* of the household as the housekeeper and maid-in-waiting" (note the euphemistic language or language of mis-recognition that Jacobs seemingly uses to speak of her aunt as a mammy).[45] In an extended passage, Jacobs vividly sketches the work-related role of mammy that Aunt Nancy fills, stating:

> She had always slept on the floor in the entry, near Mrs. Flint's chamber door, that she might be within call. When married, she was told she might have the use of a small room in an outhouse . . . But on the wedding evening, the bride was ordered to her old post on the entry floor . . .
>
> Mrs. Flint, at that time . . . was expecting to be a mother, and if she should want a drink of water in the night, what could she do without her slave to bring it? So my aunt was compelled to lie at her floor . . . she kept her station there through summer and winter, until she (Nancy) had given premature birth to six children . . . Finally toiling all day, and being deprived of rest at night, completely broke down her constitution, and Dr. Flint declared it was impossible she could ever become the mother of a living child. The fear of losing so valuable a servant by death, now induced them to allow her to sleep in her little room in the out-house, except when there was sickness in the [Flint] family.[46]

Jacobs' passage illuminates the immediate field of struggle inhabited by the "aunty"—in this case, that of her Aunt Nancy and Mrs. Flint. Aunt Nancy's niece describes Mrs. Flint as a woman "who had no sympathy [for her slaves]. They were the objects of her constant suspicion and malevolence."[47] Her attitude permeated Aunt Nancy's work environment and underlies the treatment which Aunt Nancy received during the years of her service in that household. As Jacobs suggests, her aunt's position was that of a drudge during her waking hours, the time in which she "toiled." At night, Aunt Nancy was "stationed" on the floor sleeping at the entry to Mrs. Flint's chamber to await any need of the slave mistress—a station reminiscent of that set aside for an animal, not a human being. Again, Jacobs draws a graphic picture of the symbolic violence directed at the enslaved woman, manifested in the bodily disposition and site of Aunt Nancy's sleeping arrangements. And the long-term consequence of this symbolic violence is the physical violence of Aunt Nancy's premature birthing of her children.

At another level, this passage describes the deeply embedded dispositions and practices of the culture—that is, the *habitus* of the mammy or aunty, in addition to those of violence and bodily sleeping inscription exemplified in the household as a field. The culture of the slavocracy created social patterns in which slave masters and mistresses could hold, at best, only ambiguous and equivocal feelings about their slaves. Dr. Flint could pursue Jacobs sexually and also whip her for insolence or resistance; Mrs. Flint could allow her mammy to have a wedding and then on that special evening require her enslaved woman to take her station on the floor of her chamber entry.

These dispositions and practices arose from the structuring of a society in which "slaveholders' refusal to view their slaves as ladies and gentlemen entailed more than a refusal to grant them genteel social status. It withheld minimal respect for those attributes of . . . femininity that the slaveholders most valued for themselves."[48] Elizabeth Fox-Genovese asserts that "mammy" encapsulated the normative "white views of gender roles among their servants and white anxieties about their relations with their slaves whom they tried to deprive of autonomy in gender roles as in all else."[49] In other words, the image of mammy was a reflection of white values—motherhood, nurture, and reproduction (to give to the families of slaveholders) which real mammies were expected to forego for their own children (except to the degree that such activity was necessary to produce human capital and socialization for the slave masters' self-interests).

A womanist framework enables a close reading of these practices and dispositions which reveals the critically contentious nature of this social world. Enslaved women, such as Jacobs, clearly delineate the "faithful service" provided to slaveowners' families by the mammy from the structured attitudes and practices by which slaveowners attempted to keep enslaved women from giving "faithful service" to their own children. Moreover, enslaved women in most instances found ways of nurturing and mothering their children. And they lived out self-defined gender roles when they had the opportunity to do so. Jacobs' narration about Aunt Nancy includes a poignant tribute to just such resistance. Illustrating the nature of a hidden transcript, she writes:

> She was my mother's twin sister, and, as far as was in her power, she supplied a mother's place to us orphans . . . When my friends tried to discourage me from running away, she always encouraged me. When they thought I had better return and ask my master's pardon, because there was no possibility of escape, she sent me word never to yield. She said if I persevered I might, perhaps gain the freedom of my children, and even if I perished in doing it, that was better than to leave them groan under the persecutions that had blighted my own life.[50]

These words demonstrate the ability of the mammy to "resist the temptation to capitulate to the demands [and values] of the status quo."[51] It was enslaved women's struggles for freedom for themselves, their children, and the enslaved community which constitute the third dimension of the enslaved women's work ethic.

This analysis of enslaved women's work as multiple embodied labor brings to light the complex nature of enslaved women's struggles to understand their bodies as sources of affirmation of life rather than its denigration. A womanist methodological framework arises when considering how enslaved women waged war against whites violently using enslaved bodies for physical and symbolic capital and violence. Delores Williams indicates that one such element of a womanist methodological framework is a "survival intelligence [having] to do with plantation politics of learning how to be visible and accessible while simultaneously keeping out of the way" of the slave master, his wife, and the overseer.[52] Both the narratives of Jacobs and Picquet indicate the intrigue and subterfuge necessary to be present, have reasonable excuses for being absent, and avoid opportunities of being assaulted by their masters or mistresses.[53]

Another element for consideration in a womanist methodological framework is the matter of skin color. Examination of the narratives' texts clearly identifies skin color as a "practice" and "disposition" in white and black social worlds in slavery. The narratives utilized here forcefully point to the ways in which light or "white-like" skin color was constructed in and for white practices (Mattison and the owners depicted in Picquet's narrative, Dr. and Mrs. Flint in Jacobs' narrative, and Kleckley's narrative). However, these particular narratives do not address directly the positive symbolic and cultural capital that light skin color could bring to enslaved women's lives.

As a practice and form of capital, skin color could mean access to material resources or a better work situation. For the enslaved woman whose family was broken apart in Jacobs' tale, the promise of "being treated well" alludes to the material gain such symbolic capital could bring. For Jacobs herself, such symbolic capital, while being a negative dynamic in the harassment by Dr. Flint, was also a positive symbol of the work-related roles she held in the Flint homes—both in town and on the plantation. That is, Jacobs was never an enslaved field hand. Such observations indicate the conflicting and potentially dangerous nature of the terrain of moral agency for enslaved women, the elusive nature of capital (power) for enslaved women, and the varied ways enslaved women had to "form [their] own [moral] judgements" from context to context.[54]

Everyday Tools of Moral Agency:
Enslaved Women's Use of Work Skills and Crafts

The fourth characterization of the enslaved women's work ethic is blackwomen's own work-related attitudes of self-reliance and confidence in learned craft and skill. Jacobs indicates that it is the self-reliance, the "perseverance and unwearied industry," the voluntary self-sacrifice, and her grandmother's skill as a baker and seamstress, that made her "think that freedom like her [grandmother's] was more the will of God than her situation as the property of Dr. Flint."[55] In writing her own narrative, Jacobs says that the purpose of her writing—that is, her work in freedom as a black abolitionist author, seamstress, and nursemaid—is for the public voicing of "the conditions of sister enslaved women in the South, still in bondage, suffering what I suffered, and most of them far worse."[56]

Within the narrative of Lucy A. Delaney we find a very poignant passage that relates the moral motivation and meaning of work which Polly Crocket teaches her daughter Lucy, after they successfully win a court battle reestablishing their freeborn status and recounting the events of their kidnapping into slavery:

> Her [Polly's] next thought reverted to sister Nancy. So we earnestly set our selves to work to reach the desired end, which was to visit Nancy in Canada and seek the long-lost girl. My mother being a first-class laundress, and myself an expert seamstress, it was easy to procure all the work we could do, and command our own prices. We found, as well as the white, a great difference between slave and free labor, for while the first was compulsory, and therefore, at best, perfunctory, the latter must be superior in order to create a demand, and realizing this, mother and I expended the utmost care in our respective callings, and were well rewarded for our efforts.[57]

As in Jacobs' tale, Delaney's mother is cast as the moral good and powerful woman who reclaims freedom for her children. Yet, in this passage, there is a direct movement from moral action to the moral understanding of work and labor. Work in slavery "is compulsory and, at best, perfunctory." Work done as a free person, as learned craft and skill performed with excellence and in the service of freedom for self and others, is completely satisfying and is understood as the essence of calling. Calling, in this case, was understood to mean that talent and labor was a gift from God for the building of the community.

Elizabeth Kleckley's narrative speaks plainly to the difference in the master's understanding of work and that of the enslaved. She states that "work was the slave's duty." Yet from the point of view of the enslaved, work was "self sacrifice for the purchasing of mother, myself, and my son."[58] And finally, from Aunt Sally, "The moment that [I] was free to act for [myself], with what spirit and energy did [I] take hold of life."[59]

Reports like these were prominent in interviews, articles, and newspapers. These sources mainly reported on the actions of men. However, the nature of enslaved women's work and flight for freedom was occasionally reported. From Frederick Douglass' newspaper, the trials of Katy were told. Katy, a woman of fifty years, escaped from her master in Virginia. Many years earlier, their master had beaten Katy's husband to death for his resistance to the master's sexual advances toward Katy. Douglass writes:

> The murder left Katy a widow with two girls of ten and twelve years old. It also raised up in her a determined resolution to break away and be free, and hereupon the latent energy of her nature came into powerful action. She knew that money was indispensable, so she worked and toiled between tasks that their virtuous resistance caused her master to increase in severity, and by trafficking with the negroes around accumulated a small sum. But it took twenty years to do so![60]

In that time, the daughters had grown up, become "profitable as breeders," and had been married to fellow slaves on the plantation.

After a successful escape with one of her grown daughters, son-in-law, and grandchildren, Katy returned to Virginia to buy the freedom of the daughter who had lost the courage to attempt escape. While living as a fugitive, but in freedom, Katy again worked, becoming a famous cook in a Philadelphia hotel. Upon earning three months' wages, Katy quit her job and went to Virginia. Returning to the plantation of her former master, Katy found that her daughter had been tortured by the master and forced to reveal her knowledge of the escape plot. She was still in a weakened state. The master had since died, and provisions were being made to have his chattel sold. That night Katy escaped with her daughter and two adult enslaved men.[61]

Such witnesses are the exceptional ones in enslaved women's narratives. The everyday experience of the masses of enslaved women were not concerned with the possibilities of earning money in order to purchase freedom for family members or for one's self. They were focused on the needs for survival and the immediate maintenance of self, family, and community. All the work that enslaved women did in their roles as "slaves" and as mothers, wives, daughters, and the like, was embodied work—that is, their bodies were the location of enslaved and/or liberating work. Yet, different kinds of work engaged women in different embodied or socially constructed fashions.

The sexuality, family customs, and traditional divisions of labor that Africans had been accustomed to on the continent changed dramatically in chattel slavery. Angela Davis noted, "This was one of the supreme ironies of slavery: in order to approach its strategic goal—to extract the greatest possible surplus from the labor of slaves the black woman had to be released from the chains of the myth of femininity . . . The sheer force of things rendered her equal to her man."[62] James Monroe Abbot remembers that his mother

> . . . wuz big an strong. She nevuh worked in de house none but dey wern't nothin on de place she couldn't do. She cut down trees, chop off a rail length, and use a wedge an' maul an' make rails as good as anybody. Poor Mutuh, she shore did have a hard time. Dey wer'nt nothin' her but hard work all de time. She nevuh come in fum de feel' 'til dark, den had to feed wid a lantern.[63]

Abbot's description of his mother's life is to the point concerning the division of enslaved labor. Davis is addressing the role that enslaved women played in the general production on plantations, and in that role all slaves were equal. Abbot's recollection is indicative of the negative side of that gender equality in enslaved production.

However, there were many instances when women's embodied selves became the direct target for humiliation and torture in work, especially as it related to women's attempt to get relief from the work regime. Aunt Charlotte recalls that an enslaved woman from a neighboring plantation was caught after an attempted escape. Nellie was described as having "long straight hair" and skin color that was "almost white." After capture, Nellie's hair was cut short; she was made to wear men's clothes and to work alongside men in the fields and on the levees; and they put deer's horns on her head to punish her.[64]

Nellie's punishment was inflicted upon her body in a such a way as to brutally reveal the social inscription of all enslaved women's bodies. Several elements of her identity were altered to make a public example of her (that is, a public transcript). Nellie's hair was cut short and she wore men's clothing—a sign to most people of humiliation. She was given the headdress of an animal to remind her and those who saw her that she was no better than one. Nellie was given work, perhaps as a member of a male work gang, on a river levee—a very open and, most likely, visible place. In each instance, Nellie's unsuccessful escape became a public spectacle. Her ability to be a self-defining moral agent was being publicly ridiculed.

Escape from the work regimen continued to be a pattern of agency for women—an action of self-protection and care. Deborah Gray White indicates that truancy became a favored means for women to "reconcile their desire to flee and their need to stay. Studies of female runaways demonstrate that females made the most likely truants [rather than escapees] because they were more concerned about breaking family ties."[65] Nearby woods, more isolated individual slave cabins, or the residences of free blacks often became havens for women resisting the toil of the slave labor and caring for self. For many women, it became a practiced skill and art form of resistance when they had been abused or overworked. Just as frequently, but not without danger, other enslaved women in solidarity often assisted in providing food, child care, or needed information to the truant woman. They too had a cost to pay for their moral agency if their acts of resistance were detected by slaveowners.

One of the most common forms of utilizing moral agency, skill, and craft in the everyday world of enslaved women was through the same types of work done for one's family that was done for the slaveowner and his or her family. A prime example of such typical work was the provision gardening alluded to earlier. Here is the material substance of an enslaved women's work ethic because it is an example of the fundamental work necessary for survival and maintenance of the family, while more elaborate means of survival were being devised for attaining freedom.

Nearly all women had experience in agriculture in antebellum slavery. Household servants, especially the cooks, raised garden produce for the slaveowner's table. Most women, particularly those on small plantations of under twenty slaves, worked in the fields raising cotton, rice, tobacco, wheat, or sugar, depending on their geographic location. And these women were not deceived by the anomalies of white and black labor:

> Lord, Mr. Gibson, he had big farms en my mother and my father, dey worked in de farms. Yes'um, my mother and father, I used to never wouldn' know when de come home in de evenin it would be so late . . . I don't know how long dey had to work, mam, but I hear dem say dat dey worked hard, cold or hot, rain or shine. Had to hoe cotton en pick cotton en all such as dat. I don' know, mam, but de white folks, I guess de took it dat dey had plenty colored people en dey Lord never meant for dem to work. You know, white folks in dem days, dey made de colored people do.[66]

However, it was provision plots that served the needs of the enslaved women and her family. Narrative upon narrative gives evidence of the vital importance of provision plots in the life of enslaved women. Many times these plots, along with game from fishing and hunting performed by the men, made the critical difference in whether an enslaved family would starve. Sojourner Truth's family raised tobacco and corn that was exchanged for articles of clothing or food, as the family needed.[67] Others reported that ". . . It jes lak I tellin' yunnah my Massa gi he colored peoples mos' eve't'ing de hab en den he 'low eve'y family to hab un acre of land uv dey own to plant. Hadder work dat crop in de night. Make light wid fat light'ud stump wha' to see by. Dat crop wha' de buy dey Sunday clothes wid . . ."[68] Provision gardening, together with the everyday household duties that enslaved women undertook for their families—cleaning, washing, weaving, cooking—was moral work for enslaved women to the extent enslaved women understood and chose the work for familial and community survival rather than as simply "women's (gendered) work." It ensured some measure of daily survival, nurturing, and maintenance, and it was this daily work that sustained generations from slavery even into emancipation and beyond.

Reflecting on Moral Agency and Suffering in Work

In examining the witness of enslaved women as they sought to make their lives count for more than an entry in the slaveowner's ledger, the overwhelming reality of suffering, evil, and toil cannot be overlooked. While the concern is a theological one from the standpoint of God's purposes for human life through work, it is fundamentally also a moral question. The basic premise of this study is that enslaved women had a work ethic in terms of their lives' purposes and that this ethic was, in part, the vehicle through which they acted as moral agents. Since the need for cheap labor defined the work enslaved women did within the structure of slavery and socially rendered them beasts of burden, "work" becomes problematic as a source of human fulfillment.

To wrestle with these matters, I turn again to the lives of enslaved blackwomen. Several dimensions of their moral behavior suggest insights into the dissonant relationship between the realities of work, toil, and moral agency. Enslaved blackwomen knew fundamentally that work under forced labor and living was wrong. This made the nature of the work they were required to do evil. It was evil because it grew out of the sinful human will to subjugate and exploit others in terms of individual and group self-interest. Their lives demonstrated that the result of such evil was unwarranted, unearned, and undeserved suffering which had no value or justification in terms of the institution of slavery. In coming to terms with this, enslaved women bore a legacy of African traditional cosmology. In its foundational principles, evil was understood for many African peoples to be the result of human action, or the spirit forces that inhabited the world. God, or the supreme deity, within such a cosmology was not the source of evil. Rather, it was immoral behavior and a product of the human world.[69] Evil manifested itself through the witch or the sorcerer.

Chattel slavery brought Africans and African Americans into cultural contact with western Christianity, but a Christianity used to legitimate slavery. In its teachings, moral virtues, and preaching, this Christianity upheld the power and status of the slavocracy. In doing so, enslaved women ferreted out, perhaps utilizing their African legacy, that which they knew spiritually to be lies. The words of Sojourner Truth to her slave mistress and the testimony of Elizabeth Kleckley imply the ability of enslaved women to apply a hermeneutic of suspicion to plantation Christianity. It was this hermeneutic which enslaved women appeared to apply to the exhortations of white preachers and slave masters and mistresses. In doing so, contemporary womanist ethicists and theologians recognize enslaved women's ability to discern theological doctrines and spiritual understandings that illuminate the nature of oppression, empowerment, and liberation.

Reading the life and moral agency of Louise Picquet and Harriet Jacobs sheds further light on this hermeneutic of suspicion. Picquet, with a great deal of tenacity, caught her interviewer, a Christian minister, in his ignorance about the basic essentials of slave auctions in his questioning of her:

> Q.—"Where was that [where you were sold]?"
> A.—"At the market, where the block is . . ."
> Q.—"What block?"
> A.—"My! Don't you know? The stand, where we have to get up!"[70]

Harriet Jacobs had to contend with a grandmother who struggled with an evangelical faith that seemed unrealistic in regard to the morality of enslaved women, who were forced to choose less than ideal moral actions in the face of continual sexual harassment. Elizabeth Kleckley was sold to a Presbyterian minister who was a cruel slaveowner. Such hermeneutics were necessary for survival in the midst of ethical ambiguity, the immorality of slaveowners, and the injustice of the institution of slavery.

Rather than build a theology or ethic of suffering, enslaved women developed an ethic of resistance in their response to both the reality of evil as they recognized it and the suffering that they experienced. Womanist theologian Shawn Copeland states, "As a mode of critical self-consciousness, Black women's cognitive practice emphasizes the dialectic between oppression, conscious reflection on the experience of oppression and activism to resist and change it."[71] Like the suffering that is fully embodied—whether it is spiritually, emotionally, or physically—so enslaved women's resistance is embodied.

The women of the slave narratives were able, by the treatment they received and the words they heard from slave masters and mistresses, to understand the meaning of work. In relation to exploitation, work was evil and caused suffering. In relation to resistance for self, family, and community in the midst of oppression, work was a source of faithful, moral living. Work was, in this way, about living and resisting the consequences of evil. In neither case did enslaved women seem to condone suffering. That they suffered as a consequence of trying to live in a more fully human way was costly as seen from their own perspective.[72]

When lifted up from the voice of enslaved antebellum women, a constructive work ethic begins to take shape in the interlocking elements of African American women's conflicting encounters with Christian notions of work and the concrete struggle for the ownership of their own labor, its products, and of their selves. As seen in the narratives of Sojourner Truth and Elizabeth Kleckley, for example, enslaved women were able to distinguish corrupted doctrines of God from their own experiences of a loving, protecting, forgiving, and liberating God. Toil in enslavement was understood by enslaved women as slavocracy's self-interested ideological reading of God's will. Jacobs recalled Pious Mr. Pike, the white preacher, saying, "Servants, be obedient to them that are your masters according to the flesh, . . . If you disobey your earthly master, you offend your heavenly Master . . ."[73] From these testimonies, enslaved women believed that God willed work and labor in civil and political spheres as well as spiritual freedom.

Furthermore, this constructive ethic bears the hallmarks of an African heritage of communal sensibilities or common orientations that are specifically religious and work related in principle. Moral agency in work was built through the authority of kinship networks, both sanguine and socially constructed. This moral authority was based on belief in respect for the skills, religious beliefs, and the agency of elders in their struggle for freedom of the kinship network and black community—both slave and free. At the center of these networks and community was a mutuality of caring between enslaved blackwomen for one another's growth and welfare. And, within this circle, skills, practices, and strategies were consciously taught and passed on for concrete use in attaining free status for individuals and freedom for the enslaved African American race. It would seem, then, that cooking, sewing, baking, and midwifery, as well as reading, writing and public speaking, became tools in the quest for freedom.

For enslaved women in particular, construction of a work ethic meant living through and beyond bodily sexual exploitation, the birthing of and nurturing attachment to children whom they knew would most likely be sold on the auction block, while at the same time finding ways of resistance in order to maintain their dignity. For enslaved mothers of daughters, a constructive work ethic meant teaching girls early about the dangerous wiles of slaveowners—mistresses and masters.

A work ethic of enslaved women offers a more realistic, a more complex, and therefore a more visionary foundation for understanding work as a key dimension of human life. It is a work ethic that gives meaning to human existence when grounded in the historic community of struggle for the freedom of an oppressed people. Arising as it does from the daily lived experience of enslaved women, this work ethic enriches our understanding of the communal task of theo-ethical faith and action, of bodily and sexual ownership of self and labor, and of skill and practice in livelihood. Having examined the work ethic of enslaved Christian women in the light of the structure and practices of slavery for the racialized and gendered nature of moral action and theological reflection, I turn next to explore the implication of this ethic in relation to the Protestant notions of vocation, calling, and work.

4

Whose Work Ethic?
A Womanist Reading of "A Work Ethic"
from the Bible to the United States

In the preceding chapter, the words and experiences of fugitive enslaved and ex-enslaved women were placed at the center of the work discussion, human meaning, and blackwomen's moral agency as the focus of this womanist ethical investigation. In listening to voices from between fifty-nine and one hundred and sixty-six years ago, I have attempted to discover the relationship of enslaved women's moral agency to the meaning of work in their lives. In reflecting on their words and actions, I have constructed four characteristics of an enslaved women's work ethic: 1. a theological and ethical belief in God as the God of life, freedom, and protection; 2. womanish moral authority, instruction, and action as an intergenerational dynamic for communal maintenance, solidarity, and empowerment in the context of oppression; 3. a struggle for self-determination in the use of one's labor, especially sexual and reproductive labor; and 4. a work-related attitude of self-reliance and confidence in one's learned skill and craft. I contend that these characteristics point toward a work ethic that has as its goal the move from survival to the ongoing creation of abundant life, freedom, and human wholeness in the face of and opposition to oppression and evil and the struggle for liberation.

The questions that this chapter takes up ask the meaning of enslaved blackwomen's reality in relation to Christian faith and the work ethic in light of the Christian tradition and in the ethos of

the United States. Three issues emerge. One revolves around
understanding and interpreting the Protestant social teachings on
work and vocation. Biblical perspectives, of course, lay beneath
the church's social teachings. Another set addresses the nature of
the work ethic in its development in the United States historically.
Lastly, there is the interface of these traditions with the lives and
experience of enslaved blackwomen.

Biblical and Theological Perspectives on Work

In antiquity, to work was to toil and labor under the yoke of
sustaining and reproducing human life itself. In order for human
life to exist, persons had to struggle with and/or against nature,
depending on whether one saw nature as harmonious or hostile. In
the West, nature was considered hostile to the development of
human life and civilization so that work became a precondition
of life, not meaningful but necessary. "Freedom" meant freedom
from work because work was understood to mean providing the
necessities of life. The "free" person did not work because
others—women and men slaves and women in the domestic
sphere (wives and daughters)—attended to the labors of life.[1] For
example, in the Greek city-state, the *polis,* the free person was the
citizen who engaged in the public life—politics—and the pursuit
of the virtuous or honorable life. Taking their cues from and emu-
lating the gods of their culture, free citizens were patrons of
the arts—crafts considered beautiful and more permanent than the
work of domestic life or the private sphere. Jürgen Moltmann
makes the connection between ethics, work, and slavery in antiquity by asserting that "the separation of virtue and work mani-
festly reflect[ed] a slaveholding society. . . . In it, not only is
labor exploited for the sake of profit. But rather, work itself is
understood as enslavement, that is, to 'work means to be a slave of
necessity.' "[2]
Decidedly different from the Greek tradition that has shaped
one of our conceptualizations of ethics and work are the biblical
notions of work. Work is part of the relationship between God and
humanity. There are two frameworks within the Bible in which to

view work. The first framework has three elements. First there is the work of God—creation and redemption (liberation)—which the Bible attributes to God alone and which consequently encompasses God's covenantal relationships with humanity through Israel and beyond (Gen. 1–2; Ps. 8:3; 33:6; 104:24; 148:5; Isa. 43:24ff. and Isa. 53). Second, there is the realm of human work—that is, all the work that humans do to meet our basic needs and to live socially (Gen. 1–2). Such work is necessary. By *necessary,* I mean work that is for the maintenance and reproduction of human life, mediating between our relationship to nature for the satisfaction of life's basic needs and our relationship as culture-creating-building-sustaining beings. Even "at the beginning of creation there was no work-free age . . ." and only "after the Fall is work cursed by toil, pain, and uselessness," according to Moltmann.[3] (Of course, it is important to remember that the Church has traditionally read Genesis 3 as justification for the view that Eve's sin is blamed for work becoming "toil.") Third, when the faith community and its members live and work in and for the kin-dom of God (Mark 16:20), such participation in work is a participation "in Christ." This is the metaphorical faith understanding of work, in the sense that the community of faith "works" in the cause of the Gospel or "the work of Christ" (Phil. 2:30).[4]

The second framework consists of the diverse perspectives on work within the varieties of biblical traditions. Work in its several patterns and divisions of labor in this framework is related to the different historical and economic situations of the several biblical traditions and to the ideological commitments present in those traditions. As depicted in the Pentateuch and the "historical books," human labor in Israel's nomadic and agricultural life is seen as self-supporting, communal (in the sense of extended kinship relations and within the context of community), and meaningful. This is true even when work is viewed as toil done "by the sweat of their brow" in such narratives as the story of Cain and Abel, the story of Noah and the Flood, the Abraham and Sarah cycles, and the narratives of the early confederacy period. In Exodus 1–2, the Israelites find themselves in slavery and conscripted for the public work projects by Pharaoh. In 1 Kings 5 and 9, it is clear that King

Solomon has created a forced labor system utilizing Israelites or foreigners within Israel's borders to build the Temple and the king's house. Likewise, the Prophetic literature denounces the oppression of the poor through unjust labor systems and their products (Isa. 31:3) and the idle rich (Amos 6:3–6), while the Psalter raises the concern of Israel's faithfulness through its work while the nation is in exile. Ecclesiastes and Proverbs, as examples of the wisdom literature, often commend the proper work attitude as that of diligence and care in one's labor as well as the most fruitful way of securing an identity as God's people (Prov. 6:6–11 and 12:24).

The New Testament—both Synoptic literature and epistolary works—contains multiple meanings and uses of human work. In the Synoptic parables, daily work themes and activities become the context for metaphors of the new reign of God (Matt. 13:1–23, Mark 4:1–20, and Luke 8:4–18; Matt. 20:1–16; and Luke 13:20–21). Pauline and pseudo-Pauline letters stress work and daily living, a cheerful attitude toward work, and the condemnation of idleness (Col. 3:23 and 2 Thess. 3:10–12). Further, the daily work of Christians is addressed in household codes of Paul (Eph. 6:5–9, Col. 3:22–4:1) and in the letters of 1 Timothy, Titus, and 1 Peter. They pertain to familial relationships, including the master-servant/master-slave relationship. Within the context of daily work, there is the opportunity to see one's work as a response to life rendered to God. Work for the Christian is a vocation—that is, a vehicle through which one is to be obedient to God, who is the Christian's master. In this view of work, Paul in particular is underlining the double use of the term *vocation,* or *calling.* Persons are "called" into new life by God through repentance and faith and into the life and work of the church. This is the foundation from which Christians become "workers" in whatever they do in daily, "secular" activity.

As such, biblical portraits of work are embedded in the contexts and purposes out of which biblical writers shape their witness to God and the story of the faith community's response to God. In this latter framework, the human activity of work serves as a vehicle to the larger project of the creative purposes of God in human life and the created order. The two frameworks, while distinct, together provide the possible theological meanings of work and also descriptions of human experiences of work that stand under God's judgment and upon which the faith community does theo-ethical reflection.

Womanist Reflections on the Bible, Enslaved Women, and Work

In the Protestant tradition, laity and scholars alike turn to the Bible because it serves as the fundamental source of theological and ethical reflection in two ways. It is the repository for the archetypal, generative, and organizing myths of and for the community of faith in which the community finds its memory and purpose for the past, present, and future. Furthermore, the Bible is the paramount and first source for "doing theology" for most members of the churches—the "textbook" (written and oral/aural) for conversion and faith experiences, church school education at all levels, preaching, and group and individual meditation. This is particularly true of African American Christian women historically, and it still holds true with contemporary blackwomen. Subsequently, African American and feminist liberation biblical interpretation and theologies often ground their hermeneutics of liberation in the Exodus event.[5] But why is this the case given critical studies and interpretations of the Bible from African American liberation scholars that document and demonstrate the use of the Bible as an ideological tool to foster and perpetuate white supremacy, colonialism, and the subjugation of black Americans? Why is this the case when feminist scholars have more than adequately analyzed the prevailing patriarchalism and misogyny of the biblical traditions and texts? Both groups of scholars have drawn upon a formidable array of disciplines and methods in their work. What accounts for blackwomen's allegiance to the biblical witness—an allegiance that has been neither uncritical nor unsophisticated in the face of racism, sexism, and classism in this society?

Womanist biblical scholar Renita Weems has suggested that the answer to this question is very complicated, indeed. Owing to the historical experience of blackwomen's oppression, the Bible ought to speak with existential authority to the experience, identity, and values of blackwomen, and provide a "life guide" that sustains hope and strength in blackwomen's struggle for authentic personhood. For Weems, this complex encounter with the Bible and the Christian God is a matter of understanding and "reading the text" from one's social location. At the same time, blackwomen must be cognizant and critical of the social locations of the biblical narrators in their time and the interpretative voices in the dominant culture historically and currently (including those voices within the black male and white feminist Christian community).[6]

For my purposes here, Weems advocates a blackwomen's biblical hermeneutic grounded in neither solely an African American liberationist perspective nor a white feminist analysis. Simply put, Weems offers a womanist hermeneutic that has three elements. First, it is a hermeneutic that seeks to "uncover whose voice [blackwomen and marginalized people] identify with in the Bible—female as opposed to male, the African as opposed to the non-African, the marginalized as opposed to the dominant. Second, it has equally and more precisely to do with examining the *values* of those readers and the corroboration of those values by the text."[7] Perhaps the third and most important dimension for our reading of blackwomen's slave narratives and womanist reflections on blackwomen's lives, the Bible, and work is what Weems calls the "credibility of the text" in its portrait of how human beings relate to one another. That portrait ought to coincide with the way blackwomen have experienced reality and relationships with other people and, as a text, arouse, manipulate, and harness African American women's deepest yearnings.[8]

Turning to my own blackwoman's "reading" of the Bible in relation to work, what might be said in light of enslaved women's reality and womanist reflections? The passages selected are but possible examples of the interface of enslaved women's work existence and interpretative renderings of the Bible from a womanist perspective.[9] A womanist "voice" or "reading" emerges from the interrelatedness of African American, women, and poor peoples' experiences of oppression, struggles for survival and quality of life, and movements for liberation. As such, one exemplary biblical "portrait" selected for reflection is the narrative of the Hebrew midwives acting in the midst of a continuing and intensifying situation of oppression for the descendants of Abraham and Sarah (Ex. 1:15–22 and 2:1–10).

The major issue confronting the Hebrew midwives is the first, central, and specific issue confronting anyone or group in the narrative—the question of God's identity and authority—that is, whom Israel will worship and serve.[10] Indeed, it is the fundamental question in the book of Exodus. Likewise, it is the major theological and ethical issue for Exodus. For the midwives, authority comes to the fore when Pharaoh commands, "When you act as midwives to the Hebrew women, and see them on the birthstool, if it is a boy, kill him; but if it is a girl, she shall live" (1:16). The first answer given in the narrative is, "But the midwives feared God; they did not do as the king of Egypt commanded them, but they let the boys live" (1:17). The question of God's identity and authority is answered through the action of these women, and then we learn the details. When summoned to account for their actions by Pharaoh, the midwives respond in an ironic twist of midwifery skills: "Because the Hebrew women are not like the Egyptian women; for they are vigorous and give birth before the midwife comes to them" (1:19). Unlike Pharaoh, their knowledge of their clientele is part of their knowledge as midwives. Again we are told of the result, this time a twofold result: ". . . and the people multiplied and became very strong. And because the midwives feared God, he gave them families" (1:20b–21). Although rewarding positive human action as a response to the will of God is not automatic, it does herald that life and goodness will abound according to God's purpose.[11]

Traditionally, neither African American (male) nor feminist biblical liberation interpretations include the particularity of blackwomen when "blackpeople" and "women" are their respective subjects in relation to the biblical witness in general, or in Exodus specifically. From a womanist reading, this *visible invisibility* is ironic given that Exodus begins with the action of a

particularized group of women responding to the oppression of
the Egyptian king over Israel. Yet, in the first of the three-part pro-
logue to the Exodus narrative, the midwives are women who can
be recognized by ethnicity, by class (that is, work) orientation, and
by solidarity with other women.[12] From a blackwoman's reading,
they are multiply oppressed people as Hebrews, as Hebrew
women, and as "domestic workers." They, like Moses later in the
narrative, become deliverers of their people.[13] As Hebrew women,
they are by their actions in solidarity with the Hebrew women and
their God. By what set of values and hopes do these Hebrew midwives do what they do?

The answer is that Shiphrah and Puah, who in faith, by
courage, and perhaps in commitment to their people or in solidarity with others, and with the skill of their craft, positively respond
to the God of the Hebrews and thwart the will of Pharaoh. By
doing so, they act to maintain the survival of the Hebrew people.
And they do so with no stated intention or expectation of receiving a reward. (Survival of the Hebrew people is later placed in the
hands of a male hero—Moses—and thus raises thorny sexism
issues about women's traditional female and domestic role related
to birth, children, and status in patriarchal culture, and the sub-
verting of women's subversive power!)[14] It is their "fear of God"
which compels them to risk and act. According to Cheryl Exum,
"to 'fear God' does not simply mean to be afraid of God or God's
punishment; it is, on the contrary, a far broader theological
concept, having at its center the element of *mysterium tremendum*
and extending to conduct which is guided by basic ethical principles and in harmony with God's will."[15] Exum reminds the reader
that in the wisdom literature, it is this sense of awe, "the fear of
God," that is the beginning of knowledge, a knowledge that is not
the exclusive prerogative of the Israelites.[16] In other words, one
needs right knowledge and relationship with God. Such faith and
action are not unlike the stance taken by Sojourner Truth in the
face of an arrogant proslavery woman, and Harriet Jacobs in
opposition to Dr. Flint.

Probing this resonance more deeply with the assistance of a
womanist reading of Scripture and enslaved women's narratives

can reveal an important insight. It is possible to argue that right knowledge and reflexive action on the part of the Hebrew midwives and enslaved women was more acutely faithful to an understanding of God than that of either Pharaoh or the proslavery "Christian" woman. Pharaoh thought himself to be divine and was worshiped by the Egyptians as god. Over against Pharaoh, the midwives "fear [the] God" of the Israelites. Similarly, the proslavery woman assumed she knew God's intention was the enslavement of African Americans while Truth counters with a different claim about God's identity. As it turns out, Pharaoh is no god at all, at least in comparison with the God of the Israelites, and is in fact a god of oppression and death. Likewise, it turns out that the God of proslavery Christianity is also one of oppression and death in the sensibilities of enslaved women such as Truth and Jacobs.

It is also affirmed that the God who stands in the background behind the Hebrew midwives and the One who stands behind Sojourner Truth is the God and Creator of life. This God is the One who in the creation of the cosmos creates human beings and fashions them after God's own likeness. Moreover, it is the same God who covenants with human beings (Abraham, Sarah, and Hagar's descendants) to make them purposeful people in specific times and in specific ways according to God's expanding purpose. And it is yet again this God who is able to have relationships with the lowliest in life's stations according to the world's standards, and use them for the working of God's purpose. God's work is neither fanciful nor negatively manipulative. It is a working that empowers midwives and enslaved women to act, which aids the growth and multiplication of their people, and which also has an effect on God's own possibilities.[17]

A womanist reading thus uncovers a new dimension of black-women's theo-ethical understanding of God. It appears from the dialogue between the biblical and enslaved narratives that the interaction between faithful women and a faithful God makes possible the expansive moral agency of each. Each party calls the other into greater fullness of being in a relationship in which remembrance of the past, faithfulness in the present, and just moral activity combine to affirm, defend, and perpetuate life as the divine purpose of God and the human purpose of women. On one level, the Hebrew midwives "to fear [the] God" of the Israelites is just a contrast of confidence and knowledge between Pharaoh and God. It is more than that, however. On a deeper level, for the midwives to have such a knowledge of God is also to have a knowledge of God's relationship to the ancestors of the Hebrews—Abraham and Sarah, Isaac and Rebekah, and Jacob, Leah, and Rachel. The same is true of Sojourner Truth, and particularly Harriet Jacobs. As we have discovered, both enslaved women, albeit in different ways and at different ages, join their knowledge of God to the knowledge of their ancestors and ancestral ways. For Truth, it is the connection between her mother's name, Mau Mau, and her mother's admonishment to recognize that there is but one Being greater than the then child, Isabella, the God of the universe. For Jacobs, it was the integration of the power of her parents' spirit of freedom and the power of God that launched her on her escape. The blackwomen's theo-ethical insight is that remembrance of the past, faithfulness in the present, and just moral activity by God and persons of faith together restore a degree of moral harmony in the universe.

Returning to the critical nature of the project at hand in reading the narrative of the Hebrew midwives next to narratives of enslaved women, I draw attention to the ethical nature of how women understand the work they do. In the context of Hebrew scriptures and enslaved women's lives, midwifery was itself work that affirmed life and assisted persons and communities through the human life cycle. It was a craft that was viewed as a basic medical support to women in pregnancy and birth—that is, in bringing forth new life. Ex-enslaved woman Aunt Clara Walker recounted for her interviewer, "When I was thirteen years old my ol' mistress put me wid a doctor who learned me how to be a midwife. Dat was cause so many women on the plantation was catchin' babies. I stayed wid that doctor . . . for five years."[18] Yet, midwifery was actually broader in scope. Particularly in traditional societies, midwives served as the "medicine" women of their communities and cultures, often acting as nutritionists, herbalists or rootwomen, physicians, religious ritualists, and counselors. They were teachers, healers, and communicative leaders who sought to empower the health and welfare of their clients and communities. As I implied earlier, one feature of the Hebrew midwives' craft and wisdom was that of knowing their clientele better than Pharaoh. They were women who understood the cultural and countercultural aspects of their work setting and the community. In doing so, they were able to engage in successful subterfuge against Pharaoh.

These too were often the midwife roles of enslaved women. In spite of the fact that slaveholders had a relative self-interest in protecting the health of pregnant women as well as others in one's labor force, they often cut operating expenses by utilizing midwives instead of a doctor.[19] Moreover, midwives served a vital companionship role to pregnant and postpartum women or as instructors to other enslaved women who would support the newborn and its mother on their or neighboring plantations. Especially when attending to health needs on other plantations, midwives served a vital enslaved community communications role, sharing news from one plantation to another in the respective slave quarters. Together, the nature of the work and the moral choices made by the practitioners and clients form the nexus of the moral act or activity in relation to life or death, wellness or sickness.

Given these two dimensions, the work of the midwives and enslaved women offers a critique that counters Pharaoh's understanding of work. The text tells us that military readiness, international competition, and power conditioned Pharaoh's view of work. Work was organized so that taskmasters were set over the Hebrews "to oppress them with forced labor" and to make their lives "bitter with hard service in mortar and brick and in every kind of field labor" (Ex. 1:11, 14). In a sense, the forced labor of the Hebrews was, according to Pharaoh, the appropriate work of the mass of common people (the Hebrews outnumbering the Egyptians) who labored for upper classes, the priests, and god-king. Indeed, large economic enterprises—work supporting empire-building—were connected to the state religion, its cult(s), and its gods in the ancient Near East.[20] In essence, that work maliciously exploited the labor of others, often in a death-dealing fashion. Pharaoh had sought the work of the midwives as part of his exploitative, imperial scheme, but they refused to participate in their own exploitation and that of the Israelites. Instead, they chose to place their labor—its skills and its knowledge—on the side of the Israelite God whose work would be revealed in the redemption of Israel.

As we saw in the Kleckley, Jacobs, and Delaney narratives, slaveholders and the system of slavery appropriated enslaved women's work more often than not. Yet, we also saw how their labor placed in service of enslaved individuals (especially children) and the community affirms and sustains life in the midst of oppression and in the hope of freedom. This latter work, like that of the Hebrew midwives, sought to participate in the purpose of God's work in creation and in redemption—life given by the Creator, life preserved by the Creator, and life enjoyed in the Creator. From the vantage point of the biblical and enslaved narratives in dialogical reading, a womanist understanding of work emerges that connects the work of God and the work of humanity.

Notions of "Work and Calling"

I now turn to the theological and ethical roots that gave rise to the notion of a "work ethic" in Protestant thought. The early Protestant Reformers, Martin Luther and John Calvin, gave Western thought and Christianity the first interpretation of work as a positive social act applicable to all persons in every socio-economic, political, and occupational status. In fact, these respective interpretations were intended to end what the Reformers saw as a false dichotomy between the highly privileged vocation and calling of the religious life and the lesser esteemed life of toil in the everyday world prevalent in Roman Catholic thought. Martin Luther proclaimed the recovery of "the priesthood of all believers" in the Leipzig Disputation of 1519, and in "An Appeal to the Ruling Class of German Nationality . . ." He wrote:

. . . there is no true, basic difference between laymen and priests, princes and bishops, between religious and secular, except for the sake of the office and work, but not for the sake of status. They are all of the spiritual estate, all are truly priests, bishops, and popes. But they do not all have the same work to do . . . A cobbler, a smith, a peasant—each has the work and office of his trade, and yet they are all alike consecrated priests and bishops. Further, everyone must benefit and serve every other by means of his own work or office so that in this way many kinds of work may be done for the bodily and spiritual welfare of the community, just as all members of the body serve one another [1 Cor. 12:14–26].[21]

Theologically and ethically, the godly life of monasticism was posited as the vocation of all people. Labor was part of the human condition, a necessity for individual and collective survival. However, it was affirmed as part of humanity's very vocation. Since God's call comes to every Christian, vocation (call) and work (occupation) now was seen as being a dimension of Christian servanthood in church and society. It was also a vocation for life and, indirectly as an occupation, one that lasts for a lifetime. Any attempt to change even one's indirect vocation (occupation) for Luther was seen as a disloyal, autocratic, or fanatic act.[22]

Agreeing with Luther, and expanding the notion of work as a positive human activity, John Calvin emphasized calling and vocation as demands of the Christian life, entailing obedience to God within one's calling. Calvin wrote:

. . . the Lord bids each one of us in all life's actions to look to his calling . . . he has appointed duties for every man in his particular way of life. And that no one may thoughtlessly transgress his limits, he has named these various kinds of living "callings." Therefore each individual has his own kind of living assigned to him by the Lord as a sort of sentry post so that he may not heedlessly wander about throughout life.[23]

The first goal of work was obedience to the calling of God who has given each human a calling. To be obedient in and to one's calling is, therefore, a manifestation of glorifying God. However, it was also important to Calvin that a person determine before entering an occupation, craft, or profession one's fitness to undertake it. Calvin also asserted that "Scripture leads us by the hand . . . warns us that whatever benefits we obtain from the Lord have been entrusted to us on this condition: that they be applied to the common good of the church . . . liberally and kindly . . . and are required to render account of our stewardship."[24] This was the second goal of work in Calvin's thought. Given that church and society in Geneva were one, work became a religious "duty" or obligation that enabled glorification of God and living out one's love of neighbor and one's stewardship.

Luther and Calvin believed that Christians were called to serve God and their neighbor in the everyday world, including in and through work. This affirmation gave honor and dignity to all work diligently done. "Neighbors," in Calvin's thought, even included those whom we do not know and those we consider enemies, resulting from the bond that is the human race created by God in God's own image.[25] Calvin further extended his positive valuation of work by stressing its goal—glorification of God and the building up of Christian community.

However, within each theologian's formulation exists an interrelated problem. Luther, in writing to the German nobility, maintained a rather rigid view of hereditary social status. So did Calvin. Relying on the natural law ethics embedded in their respective theologies, each believed that God assigned social and economic stations to all persons that, by implication, defined the nature of work to which one was called. Although in Calvin's thought there existed some guarded latitude in changing one's occupation, generally both he and Luther believed that any attempt to alter one's social position, and therefore one's calling, was sinful. One's calling could be exchanged only for another for the purpose of God's glory.[26] It is this rigidity that is problematic when set in relation to the later development of the notion of the work ethic. Neither Luther's nor Calvin's theology of vocation and calling ever intended to effect a different understanding or critique of the political economies of their situations. In Luther's case spiritual estates, work, temporal authority, and the economy were considered to be ordained by God and not a creation of human society. If this is believed, then not only could all work be meaningful but, by definition, even the most menial work done under the will of and for the profit of another could be just and fair work.

In Calvin's Geneva, two elements were important. First, Calvin's Geneva had been a bustling center of international trade, a site of mercantile capitalist fairs in the previous century and early part of the sixteenth century. When Calvin arrived in 1536, he found a "poor and austere city" which had seen the upheaval of war in its struggle for independence from the House of Savoy.[27] Yet, Reformation refugees from across Europe, and from France and Italy in particular, brought money, skills, and professions to Geneva during the period 1536–1560, increasing its population and reviving its export economic activities as well as its merchant fairs. It thrived on commerce rather than on manufacturing, being totally dependent on its rural peasantry and the neighboring cities of Bern and Savoy for the staples of life. Artisans and retail merchants formed the backbone of the Geneva economy. In such a situation, one was not talking about a community that was dramatically stratified, as were the nobility and peasantry in Luther's Germany. On the contrary, given the rising class status of Geneva in general, Calvin may have been addressing the question of vocation and calling from the perspective of "profession" rather than that of "labor," which may account for his greater flexibility on the matter. Furthermore, he sought to make all citizens politically aware and to instill in them a sense of public responsibility motivated by Protestant religious beliefs.

Second, Calvin's theology evoked the notion of a theocracy— the assumed responsibility to God on the part of secular and ecclesiastical authority alike, and proposing as its end the effectual operation of the will of God.[28] Calvin's conception of human society was as a Christian social organism. Hence, "the Christian society, the society which strives for earthly justice looks to divine law to be reconstituted as just, thus imitating the self's interaction with God's saving grace."[29] Thus, the work one did in the world was commensurate with the calling one did if one labored as a pastor in the church. And he further understood the church to be the model for human social interaction.[30] (In this, he differed from the understanding of the two kingdoms in Luther's thought—that is, the relationship between the church and the state and the respective role of each.) Like that of Luther, Calvin's theology understood the world as a sinful realm. However, to Calvin it was also the place where Christians were called to use their obedience in work, love of neighbor, and stewardship for the transformation of the world and in subordination to the ruling principle of God's law of love. The reality of sin necessitated, for Calvin, proactive opposition. Every member of the church, and therefore of society (a confused and often blurred distinction given the notion of "theocracy"), was to assume a social role for others through subordinating one's self-love for the love of God and others. Therefore, the meaning of work took on the added dimension of the positive effort of the redeemed community to affect the world through coordinated human effort.[31]

A Womanist Reading of the Theology of Vocation and Work

Although we can't believe or act as if the world of enslaved women was parallel or similar to that of the Reformation, a womanist reading which attends to the operations of economic structures, exploitation of work and persons, and theo-ethical critique can raise several issues pertaining to both worlds. Despite the positive affirmation of daily work as part of the Christian vocation and life, work in the theologies of Luther and Calvin is problematic.

Neither wrote from a perspective that seriously understood the economic stratification and the division of labor in which menial work was generally also exploited work. The way in which *economic relations structured economic life and work* was not their interest, and was probably not within their conceptualizations of the way the world operated. Indeed, the Fall was a fracture in society as well as in the individual. In other words, the material conditions of living—shaped by the relationship of people to production and production's role in shaping all areas of human life and structured social relations—were not an issue for theological or ethical scrutiny except as those conditions related to their concepts of the Christian in the world. In this view, poverty was not a matter of whether the economic relations themselves were just or unjust, but whether one was willing to work. Luther commented, "It is not fitting that one man should live in idleness on another's labor, or be rich and live comfortably at the cost of another's hardship, as it is according to our perverted custom. St. Paul says, 'whoever will not work shall not eat.' "[32] Calvin came closer than did Luther in understanding unjust economic "practices" such as usury and slavery, and in fact his doctrine of Christian freedom understood the Christian as one called to transform the unjust human structures of church and society. Yet both theologians maintained ancient moral ideas: "Economic behavior can be regulated by moral restraint"[33] on the one hand. They also wrestled with the ambivalence of the Christian tradition that had a concern for the plight of the poor and equally a view of the poor as those persons unwilling to work, on the other hand. Luther, a former Augustinian monk, and Calvin, a trained lawyer and academic, were both products of this tradition and history. As a result, neither theologian critiqued the class and social location in which he was embedded as to how that location shaped his notions of work and moral agency, wealth, and poverty. After all, one's class and social location was a result of the divine ordering of the world. Each of these factors seems to have contributed to a notion of work that had little regard for the reality of work as exploitation or "drudgery" and the relationship of exploited work to poverty. Instead, Calvin (and perhaps Luther) distinguished between the deserving and the undeserving poor, and maintained Christianity's traditional mixed view of the poor—that is, as Christ's brethren and as guilty sinners. The morally corrupted were those who, in the eyes of the Christian social organism, refused to work—those who were sturdy but lazy. Social control and social responsibility were comingled in Calvin's Christian social practices in Geneva, reflecting this traditional view of work and the poor.[34] However, "as time went to, business-minded magistrates began to question the traditionalist program of Calvin . . . The poor were described solely as idle and lazy, and relief degenerated to mere social control by the beginning of the seventeenth century."[35]

The coalescing of notions of work and calling as positive goods subordinated for the commonwealth in obedience to the light of God's grace seemed to be only possible in limited periods and geopolitical enclaves such as Geneva. The social theological ideals of Calvin yielded in the next generation to the growing secularization—economically and politically—of European cities such as Geneva and gave way to a new wave of the ideological use of Protestant theology. By placing an unambiguously positive notion on work as calling and vocation, as a theological belief with ethical consequences for obedience and duty without criticizing the social relations of the changing political economy, the tradition was left with no theological or moral recourse for challenging exploitative work. Indeed, because there was virtually no notions of "calling" to social transformation of unjust human structures despite the fact that such institutions were seen as the result of the Fall, little thought was given to the notion of the social structuring of work.[36] This is the incipient danger of abstracting, mystifying, and romanticizing all forms of work as theologically and morally "good." To the extent that work as "vocation" and "calling" remain abstracted from the material conditions of life and systems of exploitation, the legacy of an enslaved woman's work ethic, from a womanist reading, will critically challenge even these theological and ethical doctrinal affirmations.

The Emergence and Convergence of the "Protestant Ethic" and the "Work Ethic"

With the settling of Plymouth, Massachusetts, Bay Colonies and other Puritan enclaves in the British colonies a scant seventy years removed from Calvin's Geneva, a new generation of Calvinism transformed its theological heritage into a New World-building enterprise. Taking its forbearers' doctrine of calling and vocation, the discipline and ethic of work was the standard for ruling class women and men and laboring women and men alike. It was a discourse encompassing a religious ethical code for daily life and communal institutional life stressing the religious and civic virtues of frugality, diligence, postponement of gratification, abstinence, sobriety, moderation,[37] and stewardship. From the writings of English Puritan Richard Baxter, a vivid picture emerges of the co-joined religious and civic nature of vocation:

> The callings most useful to the public good are the magistrates, the pastors, and teachers of the church, the schoolmasters, physicians, lawyers, etc., husbandmen (ploughmen, graziers, and shepherds); and next to them are mariners, clothiers, booksellers, tailors, and such others that are employed about matters most necessary to mankind . . .[38]

This and similar themes run through the writings of Massachusetts Bay Colony Governor John Winthrop; the New England Puritan, the Rev. John Cotton; Emmanuel Downing; and later, Richard Mather.

Another root element in what would become the notion of a work ethic was taking shape roughly in sixteenth-century mercantilist Holland. Many saw this nation's growth as an outcome of its emphasis on its utilization of natural and economic resources, especially its labor force.[39] Human labor in employment, not just capital itself, came to be seen as an important source in the creation of wealth. Further, "by the early seventeenth century, especially new Protestant portions of Holland, England, Scandinavia, Germany, France, and Austria, an overtly positive attitude toward work began to emerge . . . Implicit in this redefinition of work was the assumption that it would foster the disciplines of upward mobility."[40] Thus, at least three dimensions—the religious, the civic, and the economic—served to create gradually a new ethos in the social groups positively affected by the Reformation and mercantile growth.

One group in particular, the emerging new middle class in England, formed the class that would organize the religious, commercial, and adventure-seeking endeavors in the British colonization of North America. In New England, the primary organization for colonization at first was Puritan religious freedom. The southern British colonies, especially Virginia colony,[41] began as business ventures or new life beginnings for the adventure-seekers and the indentured poor. In the former, Reformed theology and ethics were privileged, transformative elements establishing the nature of civil and economic life. This included the Reformers' emphasis on the meaning of work. Later, southern colonies emphasised settlement and the discovery and exploitation of natural resources for English economic development. The introduction of slavery, free wage, and indentured servitude, as well as notions of productivity and the rationalization of time in relation to work, were fledgling elements influencing the drive to colonize North America. Thus, notions of a work ethic grew from the confluence of religious, economic, and social transformation.

According to Mechal Sobel, Scots, Scotch-Irish, Hugenots, and "vexed and troubled Englishmen" brought with them the mixed and changing worldviews of still prevailing Medieval Catholic as well as Protestant, agrarian, and working class as well as merchant, artisan, and middle-class values.[42] Given that the colonial settlement occurred during a period of intense upheaval—familial, geographic, social, and in some cases, economic—new worldviews, values, and patterns were created and meshed with the persistence of older and traditional ones. In the ensuing religious, economic, and social life of the colonies and later the nation, a notion of a work ethic was shaped. It came to mean that "hard work, self-control, and dogged persistence" were the virtues necessary in order for most anyone to lead a successful life in America.[43]

For later historical developments of the work ethic in the United States, these religious roots legitimated the same notions of work, now joined with transvalued and transformed social and economic interests—earthly reward, class mobility, and the fulfillment of ambition—in the growing "economic democracy."[44] In this way, the use of the work ethic in the antebellum

North was an attempt to acclimate working class European immigrants into its industrial capitalism.[45] Throughout the nineteenth century, the term *work ethic* became

> synonymous with the idea of social order . . . representing a complex ethical statement of the interrelationship between the individual, what he or she produced, and society. It represented an ideal situation in which individuals received, not just payment, but ethical and aesthetic enrichment for their work as well . . . it is the idealized relationship between individuals and their labor.[46]

Embedded in this ideal work ethic were the notions of work rooted in biblical, Reformation, and Puritan ethos which understood work and labor as manual labor, craft, and mercantile entrepreneurship. According to James B. Gilbert, this "traditional work ethic depended upon the type of environment that existed in a small town or village, where each citizen could learn the values of community through the contribution of his labor."[47] This is the notion of work that Max Weber found intriguing in *The Protestant Ethic and the Spirit of Capitalism.* While the term *Protestant ethic* for Weber meant a worldview— a way of seeing one's work and life as ordered by God's call—the more modern meaning of work ethic was different. According to Ernst Troeltsch, Weber described a secularized calling that gave "rise to that ideal of work for work's sake which forms the intellectual and moral assumption underlying the modern bourgeois [industrial] way of life."[48] Not among the least important elements embedded in the secularization of the work ethic were its assumptions about individual responsibility and autonomy. Secularized as it was in the developing ethos of the United States through the industrial revolution, capitalism, and democratic individualism of the emerging nation, the meaning of work and the work ethic followed more the cultural identity of the nation than formal Protestant theology.

In the antebellum South, slaveholders' Christian ideology attempted to inculcate in the enslaved a sense of obedience to one's slave master or mistress. As for himself, the slaveowner's work ethic is no less a complicated issue than the work ethic of enslaved women. Like their northern counterparts and especially in sectional disputes, the southern planter often appealed to the same values regarding work. The classes of persons settling and planting in the South were drawn from the same English classes as were the Puritans—"pious, hardworking, middleclass, accepting literally and solemnly the tenets of Puritanism—sin, predestination, and election . . ."[49] In that sense, "the work ethic" values upheld the general American ethos about work evident at the time. Yet an attitude also existed that militated against the work ethic as derived from Puritanism. While there was a climate of interest in business and investment in and through plantation economics, that attitude was tempered by one of leisure that defined labor itself as leisurely—that is, "the first end of life is living itself."[50] Eugene Genovese takes this sentiment even further in his Marxist analysis of the "southern ethic." He writes:

> The planters commanded Southern politics and set the tone for social life. Theirs was an aristocratic, anti-bourgeois spirit with values and mores emphasizing family and status, a strong code of honor, and aspirations to luxury, ease, and accomplishment. In the planters' community, paternalism provided the standard of human relationships, and politics and statecraft were the duties and responsibilities of gentlemen. The gentleman lived for politics, not, like the bourgeois politician, off politics.[51]

Enslaved blackwomen were judged by these meanings and held morally accountable under the rubric of "obedience to your master" by the slaveholding community. However, within the enslaved and later emancipated community, ethical values and moral conduct were articulated and lived out relative to the contradictions, circumstances, problems, and possibilities within the larger race, gender, and class structures of society. This ethical construction has neither been "identical with the body of obligations and duties that Anglo-Protestant American society requires of its members," [52] nor always dependent on its basic assumptions.

A Reading of the Notion
of a "Work Ethic" through
the Lives of Enslaved Women

Having placed a blackwomen's biblical hermeneutic of reading work within the broader biblical notions of work, I now turn to a womanist examination of the "work ethic" and address two issues I see emerging from my reading of enslaved women's narratives. First, I will examine the assumptions embedded in the general notion of a work ethic by discussing social norms that are taken for granted in this notion. Second, I will raise questions about the nature of theological and ethical doctrines concerning work when associated with the learning provided by the lives of enslaved women in the antebellum.

Intrinsic to the idea of the work ethic is the assumption and privileging of labor over leisure and idleness. It implies that human activity and behavior can be understood most fully and systematically organized, or at least directed, toward a positive goal through human labor. Indeed, work itself becomes a positive moral good. In this sense, the work ethic encompasses moral action, ethical reflection, and a social ethos (inclusive of religious beliefs and/or theological views) informing the development of individuals and communities therein. Morally, the work ethic "gives a special nuance to the word 'duty' and creates an infectious model of an industrious life . . . it is not a single or simple idea. Rather, it is a complex of ideas with many roots and branches."[53]

Within these assumptions lie social and economic ones. One such assumption is that the opportunity to work, and the opportunity to achieve through work, creates personal well-being. This "opportunity" is socially and economically assumed to be normative, available, and functional for all persons or members of society at large. I argued in chapter 2 that a central goal of the New World discovery was exploitation of resources and personal achievement through economic fulfillment. It is plausible to assert that, given favorable conditions of talent, resources, and opportunity, work would lead to self-fulfillment. In such thinking, opportunity inherently means access to resources and power with which to act independently for one's own welfare and that of the common good.

There is nothing in this assumption that admits the existence of social relations of domination, subordination, or power. However, the truth is that by the mature period of the antebellum, slaveholders and the enslaved existed in relationships marked by a complex set of negotiated customs and conventions within the larger framework of domination and subordination. Slaveholders certainly had structured normative positions of dominance and power; generally, enslaved persons were relatively powerless. The enslaved lived in a relationship of enforced and reinforced dependency,[54] in the sense that their reliance on slaveholders was neither of their own choosing nor mutually defined. Considering this situation, enslaved persons' relation to work was not a relationship of opportunity, or potential achievement, or possible personal fulfillment. Their relationship to work did not come with access to the economic, social, legal, and political resources from which further access could be turned into opportunity. Independence and the opportunity to acquire power through knowledge, education, skills, tools, and economic resources are prerequisites for the possibilities of achievement and personal fulfillment attainable through work. The nature of the one-way, enforced dependency in the slaveholder-enslaved relationship (and solidified in objective structures of law, economics, and politics) reveals the near impossibility of "opportunity" as a key concept in the meaning of work in the lives of the enslaved.

A related and deeper manifestation of the notion of "opportunity" is revealed when one considers that the meaning and experience of work are *inherited* meanings and are experienced not just individually but culturally. As such, inherited meanings are resources—cultural capital—that through their operation as inheritances condition the ethos. These prerequisites to acquisition and use of power should be seen themselves as individual and/or cultural inheritances. Working with this deeper meaning of "opportunity," the notions of opportunity, inheritances, and dependency become more complex.

The slave narratives of Harriet Jacobs and Lucy Delaney speak of such inheritances. Jacobs' father, although enslaved, was considered to be a carpenter of such skill that his owner permitted him to "hire out," and even manage his own affairs with relative freedom. Jacobs' father provided his children with clothing, extra niceties, and, most important, "a feel[ing] that they were human beings."[55] Jacobs' inheritance included a meaning of relative self-esteem related to work from her father (and grandmother); the fulfillment of life's basic needs; and a knowledge of the meaning of freedom.

Lucy Delaney had been born free, and was later kidnapped and sold into slavery. Like Jacobs, she labored as an enslaved child and woman. However, she had not been taught as a child to work—for example, she was not taught the domestic arts of sewing, laundering, cooking, and housekeeping. (As an enslaved child, she had been a nursemaid.) Nevertheless, like Jacobs, she had an inheritance of the meaning of freedom that empowered her in her flight for freedom.

Both these enslaved women inherited different meanings and experiences from their families regarding work, legal, and relative freedom, and knowledge and skills upon which opportunities could be sought and created. Their experiences exemplified the relative maneuverability of the dominated who had access to the resources valued by society (but not intended for the enslaved) that could be used as leverage for opportunities. They were, however, not the norm for most enslaved women. Most enslaved women did not have parents or grandparents who were freeborn or freed. Most enslaved women were not in a context where they could become literate. Indeed, they were forbidden to gain the skills of literacy by law. Moreover, most enslaved women were not in a position to utilize what marketable skills they had to hire themselves out to earn money or to live relatively independent lives. As noted by William Harris, "By confining slaves to unskilled, rural tasks requiring no formal education or training, slavery, it is said, left blacks unprepared for any productive role in the growing cities of the nation."[56]

It would seem, then, that in situations of group dominance and subordination such as slavery, enforced dependency remains the

normative structure to thwart truly meaningful work as viewed by
the dominate social and economic norm. At the same time, it
seems equally true that there did exist those among the enslaved
those who gained relative opportunities, knowledge, and skills,
and so gained a small measure of distance from the vicissitudes of
oppression. This would involve a relative ability to influence the
powerful, but rarely the opportunity to exercise consistent power
from a structured position so as to be able to represent the
enslaved. Such situations gave an individual "influence," and
perhaps was a contributing dynamic to the development of intra-
group socioeconomic class relations and divisions, as well as the
racialized class relations between dominant and subordinate
groups.

Another underlying assumption embedded in the work ethic is
that no matter what the nature of the work and of the person who
does it, all work and all workers are equally valued. But enslaved
women's narratives, and related materials, indicate that this assumption is not true. Aunt Sally, the fugitive slave who returned to
hire herself out and purchase her freedom when her slaveowner
was in financial trouble, recalled that hiring oneself out brought
the accusation of being uppity and uncontrollable as a slave. She
understood that it was not a good thing for a slave to look self-
reliant and independent.[57]

It is clear that when work is considered valuable in itself and as a
crucial element of positive human identity, it is contradicted in
exploitative, objective structures like chattel slavery. According to
C. Vann Woodward, an historian of southern culture, notions about
the meaning and value of work ranged from subsistence farmers'
need to feed and clothe themselves to the middle- and upper-class
farmers who associated work with one's hands as indicating a
degraded status in society. He writes, "Much [of the] work in early
America required of all people was crude and hard, and little of it
anywhere could honestly be characterized as stimulating, creative,
or inherently enjoyable. Those who wrote of its joys and rewards
probably had a larger share of work that could be so characterized
than those who failed to record their impressions."[58] Woodward
also indicates that "neither the hired man nor the slave (who gen-

erally did the same work) shared the dignity and honor conferred by myth on the yeoman."[59] In either case, the contradiction in the value and meaning of work was not lost on enslaved persons. The awareness of this contradiction was captured in a slave song:

> Missus in the big house,
> Mammy in the yard,
> Missus holdin' her white hands,
> Mammy workin' hard.
> Missus holdin' her white hands,
> Mammy workin' hard.[60]

This contradiction further unfolds. On the one hand, enslaved women (and men) knew their owners valued their work. On the other hand, the work done by most enslaved people was manual work—work that according to Woodward was "crude and hard." It was work that had historically been done under the will and for the profit of another. Enslaved people knew that they were as valuable as any property owned by a slaveholder. Yet, it was also abundantly clear that as slaves they were instruments of production and were considered tools. They were the "things" that were bought and sold to do the kind of work understood to be drudgery and toil. They knew that slaveholders generally believed, socially and religiously, that the work slaves did was the work they were created by God to do. Recalling Moltmann's words, "work itself was enslavement . . ." This double meaning of identity and work was not lost on the enslaved. Elizabeth Kleckley records witnessing her first slave auction when she was seven years old, writing, ". . . master had just purchased his hogs for the winter, for which he was unable to pay in full. To escape embarrassment it was necessary to sell one of the slaves. Little Joe . . . was selected as the victim . . . He came in with a bright face, was placed in the scales, and was sold, like the hogs, at so much per pound."[61]

Kleckley's recollection is sobering. It captures the contradiction of slavery and enslavement in an economic and social environment with deeply held biblical, Reformation-Puritan, and democratic foundations. It is no surprise then that the investigations of enslaved peoples' lives have focused not on the meaning of work as exemplified in traditional formulations of "the work ethic" but on how they lived their lives beyond their work. This chapter has placed in perspective the sweep of custom, religious faith and tradition, and historical events in the development of political economy regarding notions of work and calling, and has suggested an interpretation of the work ethic from the perspective of enslaved African Americans. It has called into question the simple historical and theological romanticization of the Reformation (and its latter Calvinist-Puritan) notions of work and calling and the secularized "work ethic" in the nineteenth and early twentieth centuries in America. Reading the notion of a work ethic from a womanist perspective on the lives of enslaved women, while maintaining that there existed an enslaved woman's work ethic, is thus at best a historical and theological paradox. At worst, the notion of a work ethic still plagues theological and socioeconomic sensibilities of African American women descendants of the enslaved in our struggle for quality of life, freedom, and liberation. The question that remains for the final chapter is how the current public debate about the need for a renewed work ethic and the clues from the lives of enslaved women stand in tension in our contemporary situation.

Conclusion

Same Ol', Same Ol' or Possibilities for a Different Future

In the nearly one hundred-forty years since the end of slavery, African American women's relation to work has been paradoxical at best and contradictory at worst. According to economist Julianne Malveaux, "Though black women's work history has been a history of steady labor force participation, black women's work legacy has been low-paid, unstable work in the service sector. Though the status of black women has changed, the inequity that has tinged the work experience of black women remains the fruit of this legacy."[1] Racism, classism, and sexism have always been interrelated in African American women's work history and legacy. These interlocking oppressions have made the gains over the last century and a half a hollow victory in black-women's—and the black community's—struggle for quality of life, against oppression and exploitation, and for freedom for self and community. As workers, familial caregivers, and community activists, blackwomen have made their way in the marketplace as "slaves," and later as domestics in servile relationships to white people and white institutions. They have shouldered agricultural, factory, educational, social service, and office work. Blackwomen have become policymakers, administrators, and entrepreneurs in the public and private sectors and have made inroads into nontra-ditional employment. As a result, African American women's work has taken place in a growing multitiered system and include

(1) those who are employed in nontraditional jobs, (2) those who work in typically female professional jobs (teaching, nursing, and social work), (3) those employed in female clerical jobs, (4) those who marginally work in service and private household jobs, and (5) those who revolve between work and public assistance.[2]

Therefore, this social history is complex—described, in part, by the nature and experience of blackwomen's work in enslavement. However, what is evident for anyone who reads that history and looks beyond the moral discourse of current public policy in relation to African American women is this fact: Beyond a doubt, blackwomen have been exemplary moral agents exhibiting a profoundly important work ethic. Birthed in pre-colonial African religious, cultural, and economic tradition, transformed in enslavement through "slave Christianity," and matured in freedom, this work ethic has stood the tests of chattel slavery, legal disenfranchisement from the economic and political rights guaranteed by the Constitution, and reversals of the gains made as a result of Executive Orders[3] and the landmark Civil Rights Acts of 1964 and 1965. All along this journey, African American women have faced personal, cultural, and institutional discrimination as enslaved women and as the descendants of enslaved women. As a testimony to the human spirit, they have maintained a critical sense of the meaning of work and its value to their communities and to Christian faith in the context of our society.

Today, this testimony persists in the midst of the public discussions surrounding the changing nature of work in our society—discussions among and about those who have work, those who do not have work, and those whose work is meaningless drudgery and goes unrecognized, unrewarded, unremunerated, and unfulfilled in ours and in the global economy. This testimony also persists in raising the question about the future of work and its implications for the increasing chasm between those who have wealth and those who are poor in the American context. In a real and tangible sense, the struggle begun in nineteenth-century America is no longer about chattel slavery but about the reality of "neo-slavery"—forms of economic exploitation and economic exclusion on the basis of race, gender, class, disability, and political affiliation. In ordinary language this struggle and its attending debate are captured in the term *jobs.*

Jobs have become synonymous with "work," and "jobs are never just jobs; they are social markers of great real and symbolic value."[4] Jobs are about material survival and comfort, employment/underemployment/unemployment, and economic advantage. Embedded within them are various ideologies of power and social relations, personal identity, talent, craft, and the role and use of technology. At the geopolitical and macro-economic level, jobs are a mediating dynamic of the relative power of nation-states, corporations, global trade, migration, and immigration—particularly to the U.S. To most of us on a daily basis, jobs (or the lack of them) are about today's realities and tomorrow's hopes and aspirations. Each of these aspects reflects objective and subjective characteristics of the nature of work—that is, objectively work is connected to the larger project of building society, to the technology developed to support this project to the actual products of labor, and to the organization of social relations through work. Subjectively, work is the actualization or fulfillment of the person who works (and the community to which she belongs). In other words, work is generative of our identity as human beings.

"Present-and-futurework," a phrase given to current and antici-pated "trends and challenges for work in the twenty-first century"[5] by the U.S. Department of Labor, Bureau of Labor Statistics, indi-cates that there are five factors driving the creation of jobs and the scale of workers' wages:

1. *Technological change:* Technological change has increased the demand for highly skilled workers in all industrialized countries, despite significant differ-ences with regard to trade, labor market institutions, and unemployment. At the same time, technological advances have meant that some lesser-skilled jobs have been replaced by new automated devices. Highly skilled workers are at a premium when new technologies are introduced because such workers are better able to use them;

2. *Trade:* Expanded trade, while opening up new markets for goods and services, can drive down the wages of low-skilled workers because it displaces the goods they produce;

3. *Immigration:* Immigration has increased significantly since 1965, particularly among less-skilled workers with lower education levels, causing greater competition for unskilled jobs and lower wages for unskilled workers;

4. *Reduced value of minimum wage:* The decline in the real value of the minimum wage and declining unionization also have contributed to the decline in earnings for low-wage workers. The federal minimum wage declined considerably in real value during the 1980s because it remained fixed at $3.35 per hour despite price increases. After having reached a postwar peak in 1968, the minimum wage fell in real terms during both the 1970s and '80s, reaching a level in 1990 significantly below its 1960 level. Failure to raise the minimum wage during the 1980s left low-wage workers further behind. (The minimum wage was increased in 1990 to $4.25 per hour, in 1996 to $4.75 per hour, and in 1997 to its present figure of $5.15 with a sub-minimum wage of $4.25 for workers under 20 years of age during their first 90 consecutive calendar days of employment with an employer);[6] and

5. *Declining unionization:* Declining unionization in the 1980s also has contributed to increased wage inequality. The American labor movement has always had a goal to help workers earn more and thereby gain access to the middle class. With declines in union membership, fewer workers benefited from the higher wages typically achieved through collective bargaining. The impact is probably the greatest on men, whose union membership rates in private sector employment fell by 50 percent between 1973 and 1993.[7]

For the African American community, an overall lack of access to quality education, skills training, career and job networks, and technological innovations has come to determine present and future work prospects *systemically,* not just in the lives of individuals. It is these systemic factors—based on race, gender, and class—that perpetuate "neo-slavery" which belies the apparent progress suggested by African Americans' incremental gains in material wealth and socioeconomic enfranchisement. The perpetuation of "neo-slavery" therefore also belies the notion that the dominant cultural work ethic in the United States has any necessary or direct connection to the larger ideals of liberty and justice for all.

The work, the work ethic, and the quality of moral agency demonstrated by enslaved Christian blackwomen become part of a dialectic through which we can begin to articulate *both* the means and the ends of justice and liberation for African American women. The means enslaved women employed in the task of doing justice and striving for liberation included, but were not limited to, their dedication to the survival of the African American community, their struggle for emancipation from bondage, and their insistence on the freedom to be a self-determining people. The ends toward which these means pointed were the preservation of blood and extended kin relations—including the preservation of the self within this network of relations—and the community-building necessary for the nurture of individual and group life. Therefore, in striving toward these ends, an enslaved Christian blackwomen's work ethic encompassed the following:

1. blackwomen's theological and ethical understanding of the relation of God to slavery as the God of freedom, shelter, protection, and abundant life;

2. womanish moral authority, instruction, and action as an intergenerational dynamic for community maintenance, empowerment, and solidarity in the context of oppression and inclusive of the coalition work of racial/gender/class boundary-crossing;

3. blackwomen's struggle for self-determination in the use of one's own embodied labor, especially sexual and reproductive labor; and

4. blackwomen's work-related attitudes of self-determination, and confidence in one's own learned craft and skill for individual and communal freedom.

Again, I define a "work ethic" as a motivating vision of livelihood—the creation and use of intuition, skills, and practices that allow for the preservation of self and family, and that contribute to the process of liberation from oppression for one's self and one's community of accountability. Together, these four characteristics suggest that the nature and meaning of work itself is found in the dialectic quest for concrete freedom and human wholeness in the face of socially constructed oppression and evil.

What difference does the moral agency and work ethic of enslaved blackwomen make to the larger religious and ethical enterprise of giving meaning to work? Moral agency is presupposed by the notion of work in the Protestant tradition and in the secularized work ethic of U.S. culture. As such, the moral agency of enslaved women—and groups like them who experience exploitative work and subhuman conditions—is a form of moral agency generated from within the material conditions of oppression and exploitation that result not from an aberration of this normative work ethic but rather as a consequence of it. It is precisely this critically important recognition that is lacking in the notion of work in traditional and contemporary Christian social ethics. Until recently, Protestant Christian social ethicists have formulated notions of work that left the material conditions of life unexamined as factors shaping the structures in which and through which people act. Instead, Christian social ethicists have opted for notions of work as theological and ethical abstractions (or doctrines) divorced from the exercise and consequences of power embedded in concrete social relations. When issues of power have been considered, they have generally been presented in a static model that has neither problematized nor demystified the social relations of domination in theological, economic, and social constructs of work. Other concrete and alternative notions of work, social relations, and power have rarely been investigated. The result has been that notions of work grounded in the concrete structures governing the division of labor and the distribution of economic resources—the means by which people meet their basic human needs and by which they participate in life-shaping and community-forming institutions—has been rendered morally suspect because of its presumed ideological bias.

Such is the case with recent and recurring so-called welfare "reform" policies at federal and state levels. The debate over public entitlements for the poor is usually staged in language that portrays the apparent lack of a work ethic as a black, racialized behavior problem rather than as a consequence of systematic poverty.[8] In her analysis of this policy reform, Traci C. West reminds us that the concepts of racialized gender and class and gendered class and race are interlocking systems for the assignment of rewards and status in our nation, which act to re/enforce and re/inscribe the economic, political, racial, and gender superiority and supremacy of whites. In public moral discourse about the working and unemployed poor, West contends that "unfortunately the 'goodness' of whites/whiteness is often only understood in converse relationship to the 'badness' of blacks/blackness."[9] The perpetrators of the moral and economic "badness" are portrayed as lazy blackwomen or "welfare queens." In essence, black parenting generally and black motherhood specifically are valued little if at all in the context of the dominant U.S. society.

The workfare requirements of the current policies often are termed "work first" requirements—that is, welfare recipients are required to participate in work-related activities in order to retain assistance for an interim period before being removed from public assistance. Such policy provisions emphasize "that any job is better than no job, urging and requiring parents [to] accept any available job. Typically this has been accompanied by a curtailment of access to education and training programs."[10] Thus, the explicit moral discourse in the political slogan of the 1996 Personal Responsibility Act was "A Hand Up Is Better than a Hand Out." The implicit metaethical and metapolitical message was

"Work (*any* work) Is Redemptive."[11] Are we, through our public policy, reinscribing "the work ethic" as *a neo-work ethic* that becomes yet again a catch-22 for the working poor and unemployed, and in particular, for African American women who need public assistance, job training, child care, and meaningful work? Are we as a society requiring more of them in order to prove their worth in society and assume the responsibility of moral agents in and through work as demanded by society?

Enslaved women's moral agency in relation to work suggests that it is unwise for theological ethics to address work in such a way that it does not maintain the tension between work as creative human production and work as exploitation based on the sinful misappropriation of power. Not all work can be called "good." The evil of exploitative work is real, and the struggle to overcome the resulting oppression is real. We are mindful of these realities when we recall that work is an *embodied* activity. Being mindful of embodiment assists us in distinguishing "good" work from "bad work." In enslavement, as in neoslavery, bodies are human capital that also carry social and cultural capital and that, as such, can be both positively and negatively valued.

This insight is particularly compelling in light of enslaved women's narratives. Work and moral agency cannot be meaningful characteristics of blackwomen's humanity in the absence of an analysis of their concrete self-determining labor, especially their reproductive and sexual labor. Enslaved women were cast into the enforced roles of sexually promiscuous beings, of breeders of enslaved human capital, and of surrogate mothers. They cared for the children of the dominant society first, and only afterward were they allowed to nurture their own children. In these and other ways described, enslaved women knew that their bodies as well as their souls bore the brunt of dehumanizing work. They understood all too well the meaning and cost of moral agency as an *embodied* state as they struggled to maintain families who could be sold away from them at any moment. Along with their men, even their bodies were counted for purposes of proportional Congressional representation in a democratic system that constitutionally maintained their disenfranchisement. Because of the varied and interrelated experiences of enslaved women that cast their bodies, by turns, as women, mothers, surrogates, sexual objects, breeders, and laborers, womanists cannot separate these forms of embodied labor. Concomitantly, enslaved women's experience of work must be distinguished from that of enslaved men. Harriet Jacobs said it directly and forcefully: "Slavery is terrible for men; but it is far more terrible for women."[12] These roles of status have deeply affected the resources available to generations of blackwomen, their families, and their communities. Thus, this experience of embodied moral agency in the midst of oppression offers significant insights and carries profound implications, yet to be fully articulated and understood even in the womanist ethical community. In light of the legacy of enslavement, embodied integrity and dignity in relation to work must necessarily be considered as a component of moral agency and work.

There are other clues from the work ethic and moral agency of enslaved women that help us to reflect on our contemporary situation. Received notions of moral action have shied away from concrete critique of social projects, programs, problems and their assessments, and instead, remained in the realm of ideal moral action.[13] In doing so, additional levels of social and political exploitation go undetected or are trivialized. For example, the nature of the violence (physical, sexual, economic, spiritual, emotional, and psychological) deployed against enslaved women (as well as men and children) by slaveholders was considered too vulgar for public discussion in northern abolitionist circles.[14] The result was that normative religious social ethics could discuss only the stated intent of *ideal* moral action and not the real suffering that the violent, immoral actions of slaveholders inflicted on their victims. Thus in broad terms slaveholders could morally justify corporal punishment as a means to achieve submissiveness as the appropriate behavior from enslaved people without the fear of having to respond to questions about their use of violence or sexual coercion in interactions with enslaved women.

Another of our pressing contemporary issues is the inequity of the criminal justice system. While we tend to focus on crime—particularly violent crime—victims' rights, and retributive punishment as the normative consequence of "justice," there is another dimension of the criminal justice system that is affected by work, the work ethic, and economic expansion. This small but growing institutional phenomenon is referred to as "prison labor," "prison slavery," "convict leasing," or "convict labor." Prison labor is rooted in the Thirteenth Amendment, which abolished chattel slavery, but which legalized the forced labor of prisoners and provided the precedent for contemporary policies toward prison labor. A series of post-Reconstruction laws, the Black Codes, empowered law enforcement officials to imprison African Americans on dubious charges of loitering and breaking curfews. These prisoners often were used for plantation and factory labor, a work existence that was all too reminiscent of slavery.[15]

By 1995 prison laborers annually produced over \$1 billion in goods and services, and the number of prisoners employed grew from 31,000 in 1990 to 75,000 in 1995.[16] It is important to acknowledge that the institutional injustice of the criminal justice system presents a web of complex problems greater than can be addressed here. That said, it is important to note that prison labor is a reemerging issue related to the future of work in this nation and to the persistence of racism, classism, and sexism. Angela Davis, working with the Sentencing Project, notes that there are in excess of 827,440 young African American males (between twenty and twenty-nine years of age) and a smaller but growing number of African American females under the supervision of the criminal justice system in the United States.[17] She sees the control exerted by corporate capitalism over the lives of people of color and poor people through prison labor as an issue connected to "civilian" job loss, general public indifference toward economic exploitation, and the undermining of unionized labor. The restructuring of the job market in response to corporate demands for cheap labor through prisons parallels the flight of capital and jobs to the Third World. Moreover, it does double economic violence to many of the same people who could not find viable, meaningful, and legal employment in the world beyond the walls of our nation's prisons. Davis calls the convict laborer "The New American Worker," a term taken from a statement by Michael Lamar

Powell, a prisoner in Capshaw, Alabama, who recognized the cruel ironies of his condition in light of the legacy of slavery, institutional acceptance of exploitative work, and the relation between race and the criminal justice-corporate capitalism axis.[18]

A womanist reading of enslaved women's lives reveals other alternatives for the grounding of moral agency that are consistent with an African American rendering of Christian faith and experience. These alternatives suggest the occasion for renewed, critical discussion within the black Christian theological and ethical community about the meaning of work in our present situation. These formulations advocate that moral agency should not be grounded in abstract ideals of moral action. Rather, they should be grounded in concrete norms and criteria drawn from a dialectic between the authoritative witness of Hebrew-Christian Scriptures and critical analysis of specific, historical experience through an assessment of the material conditions of life.

Moral agency must be understood as grounded not only in historical experiences but also in understandings of the production of work and its meaning through changing material conditions. In other words, across different historical eras as well as in everyday life, we shape and are shaped by economic relations and work patterns, not according to abstract ideas about these relations and patterns but according to lived experience. Enslaved women's narratives describe work in relation to their material conditions and the consequences of these conditions for everyday life. Economic relations and work patterns are *not* seen as created by God or by the invisible hand of the market. They are seen for what they are—human artifice—not as universals or absolutes which humans cannot alter. These insights resonate with the multidimensional historical presentations of human work and labor in Hebrew and Christians scriptures and with theological conclusions about God's work in the world through grace, redemption, salvation, and liberation. Such historical re-visioning of our notions of work and the contemporary task of biblical-theological-ethical discernment is greatly needed. The tasks implied in this critique are especially timely, given the rapid change of the structures that determine the material conditions of the lives of billions through the globalization of capital, production, and labor.

A further imperative derived from enslaved women's moral agency is that work can have value and meaning only insofar as its value and meaning derive from meeting basic human needs in community. Enslaved women (and men) understood that work was meaningful when it directly responded to the basic human needs of the enslaved community. The criteria for meeting these needs included the maintenance and enhancement of authentic community, resistance to oppression and/or empowerment for emancipation, and the opportunity to use one's learned skills for ends greater than oneself. This understanding of work places positive human relationships in community at the core of meaningful work. For example, provision gardening done by enslaved women often provided needed dietary supplements to ensure adequate health—or to stave off starvation—for one's enslaved family and community.

A more audacious conclusion underlies these observations: The experience of work and the moral agency of enslaved women (and men) suggest that work is not the primary, nor even predominant, defining characteristic of what it means to be human, even if it is critical to our sense of identity and our ability to create our world. "Religion and spirituality are more basic tools and characteristics of survival and self perception than is work for most black Americans. Through religion, there is the actualization of human being, human living, and human becoming."[19] Slave religion was the experience of being totally who you were before a very personal and present God. It was an experience of being known by this God, an experience of seeing whom and what God intended you as a person to become.

Particularly in black religion, more than denomination or faith tradition, the *community* of faith is the site where individuals and social groups shape work-as-human-meaning. It is in black religious communities that meaningful human work for many blackpeople, and especially blackwomen, is an inherited legacy, a disposition, and a practice. We see this in the fact that the black church or masjid is often the first and primary location where women and men receive the motivation to improve themselves, their families, and their neighborhoods and the encouragement to have pride in the creation and preservation of African American culture. Religious organizations within these communities of faith often provide the leadership training and skills enabling women and men to become effective public speakers, community organizers, and responsible stewards of financial resources. Guilds and fraternal/sororal orders often provide the only environment in which persons who have menial, low-wage jobs, can find affirmation; within their religious community these persons hear the important words, "That was a job well done."

For these reasons, our participation with God in God's act of creative work must be carefully interpreted when we heed the impulse to make general theological-ethical statements. The work performed in enslavement (and in contemporary exploitative work) for the profits and power of unjust institutions cannot and should not be seen as inherently good work. Nor should it be seen as co-creative work with God. Perhaps formerly enslaved woman Charlotte Brooks, speaking in an interview, best articulates this faith experience:

> Many times I have bowed down between the cane-rows, when the cane was high, so nobody could see me, and would pray in the time of war! I used to say, "O, my blessed Lord, be pleased to hear my cry; set me free, O my Lord, and I will serve you the balance of my days." I knowed God had promised to hear his children when they cry, and he heard us way down here in Egypt.[20]

Enslavement was the context of formative religious practice and profound ideological struggle. Charlotte Brooks reminds us that such struggle and practice is co-creative work with a liberating God who acts in human history. This work is therefore meaningful and a site of moral agency.

The challenge that emerges from this investigation is that religious ethics at its core should be the doing of and reflection on *solidarity* as part of faithful participation in Jesus Christ's work of redemption. Our Christian ethics should be done in conversation with those who bear the brunt of exploitative and oppressive work. In fact, the conversation about work and human meaning must be guided by workers, with theologians and ethicists serving only as facilitators and acting as members of the community of faith in solidarity with those dehumanized by exploitative and oppressive work. Of all the wisdom an enslaved women's work ethic can offer normative Protestant Christian social ethics, the most important insight is the last. It is offered to those in African American religious traditions, Christian and otherwise, and to those in the North American churches.

From the work and moral agency of enslaved Christian women, we learn that a work ethic ought not to find its root in universals or economic abstractions. Rather, meaning emerges from the interaction of persons intergenerationally and within a concrete historical, cultural, economic, political, and social situation. We further learn that within these bounded situations the differences between us can become sources of empowerment; transcendence emerges where particularity flourishes. Enslaved women perceived work as "productive" and "fulfilling" when it contributed to the community by affirming the interdependence of self and self-in-community in the ongoing struggle for emancipation and freedom. When we use our labor to meet material needs, we realize our true humanity and enable our participation with God as co-creators.[21]

Based on the testimony of enslaved Christian moral agents, a womanist theo-ethical reflection suggests this: Community/communion is the source for and the vocation of work. Both individuals and the community must respond to this vocation, together defining the nature and purpose of work in recognition of interdependence. Then we do our work, individually and together, and critique the products, processes, and institutions our work creates both in the present and in the future. Community/communion is created/re-created as the result of work. And what is faith in God but the fullest expression of authentic community/communion? This is the definition of work we hear when we listen to the voices of enslaved Christian women.

Notes

Preface

1. I use the term *blackwomen* as a more accurate social construction of identity than *black* as a mere adjective. It denotes the interrelationship between and inseparability of the experience of race and gender as interwoven social constructions. See my article, "The Notion of Difference for Emerging Womanist Ethics: The Writing of Audre Lorde and bell hooks," *The Journal of Feminist Studies in Religion,* Spring 1993, p. 39.

Introduction

1. Kwok Pui Lan, *Discovering the Bible in the Non-Biblical World* (Maryknoll, N.Y.: Orbis Books, 1995), p. 1. Here, Kwok is drawing on the work of Paul A. Cohen, *Discovering History in China: American Historical Writings on the Recent Chinese Past* (New York: Columbia University Press, 1984), p. 7. I am indebted to Kwok for the influence and appropriateness of postcolonial thought in my own work given the African American experience is the result of European colonialism in Africa.
2. See Hazel V. Carby, " 'On the Threshold of Woman's Era': Lynching, Empire, and Sexuality in Black Feminist Theory," *Critical Inquiry* 12 (Autumn 1985), pp. 262–77.
3. See Delores S. Williams, *Sisters in the Wilderness: The Challenge of Womanist God-Talk* (Maryknoll, N.Y.: Orbis Books, 1993), p. xii and Preface, note 3 for her rendering of the term "colonization of the female mind and culture."

Chapter 1: Unearthing and Remembering

1. Bethany Veney, *The Narrative of Bethany Veney—A Slave Woman* (Worcester, Mass.: George Ellis, Publisher, 1889); reprinted in *Collected Black Women's Narratives,* The Schomburg Library of Nineteenth-Century Black Women Writers, ed. Henry Louis Gates, Jr. (New York: Oxford University Press, 1988), p. 11–12; 13–14.
2. Ibid., Preface.
3. The use of the slave narratives, ex-slave narratives, and interviews has been criticized by historians for their value as objective sources. With the antebellum narratives there are several issues, including the

abolitionist ideological bias, authorship pertaining to those dictated to whites serving as editors or writers, and the matter of the class, relative privilege, and education of the authors as representative of the general enslaved population. Moreover, with the antebellum, WPA and FWP narratives, there is a decisive underrepresentation of women's voices (only 12 percent) and of narratives from the lower South. The WPA and FWP narrative interviews have further problematic aspects. Many of the interviewers were whites whose relationships to the informants exhibited the racial biases, social relations, and even local, former slaveholding histories or postbellum tenant farming arrangements. The reliability of memory is another issue since those interviewed were as young as 80 and as old as 102 years in age. Their age would also indicate that at the time of slavery the interviewees were children or adolescents with limited life experience of enslavement. Linguistic differences in African American and white southern dialect poses yet more concerns.

However, detailed reading across the different forms and periods in the narrative collection does present a fuller picture, pattern, and tapestry of antebellum enslaved life from the worldviews of the enslaved. When used with collaborative sources, this material is invaluable. For an in-depth discussion, see John Blassingame, "Using the Testimony of Ex-Slaves: Approaches and Problems," *Journal of Southern History* 41 (1975), pp. 473–92; Paul D. Escott, "The Art and Science of Reading WPA Slave Narratives," in *The Slave's Narrative,* ed. Charles T. Davis and Henry Louis Gates, Jr. (New York: Oxford University Press, 1985); and Norman R. Yetman, "The Background of the Slave Narrative Collection," *American Quarterly* 19 (1967), pp. 534–53.

4. Marion Wilson Starling, *The Slave Narrative: Its Place in American History,* 2nd. ed. (Washington, D.C.: Howard University Press, 1988), chapters 1 through 4.

5. The Northwest Ordinance of 1787 had prohibited slavery from expanding into the region north of the Ohio River. And later the 1820 Missouri Compromise did the same for a significant portion of the Louisiana Purchase. See Howard McGary and Bill E. Lawson, *Between Slavery and Freedom: Philosophy and American Slavery* (Bloomington, Ind.: University of Indiana Press, 1992), pp. 19–21.

6. Kate Drumgoold, *A Slave Girl's Story—Being an Autobiography of Kate Drumgoold,* Brooklyn, N.Y., 1897; Reprinted in *Six Women's Slave Narratives,* The Schomburg Library of Nineteenth-Century Black Women Writers, ed. Henry Louis Gates, Jr. (New York: Oxford University Press, 1988), p. 3.

7. Ibid., p. 3.

8. Lucy A. Delaney, *From the Darkness Cometh the Light, or Struggles for Freedom,* St. Louis, 1891; Reprinted in *Six Women's Slave Narratives,* The Schomburg Library of Nineteenth-Century Black Women

Writers, ed. Henry Louis Gates, Jr. (New York: Oxford University Press, 1988), p. 50.

9. Starling, *The Slave Narrative,* p. 1.

10. Ibid., xxiv.

11. John Blassingame and Charles T. Davis, "Editors' Preface," in Starling, *The Slave Narrative,* p. x.

12. Studies of slave resistance in the 1950s with the publication of Kenneth Stamp's *The Peculiar Institution: Slavery in the Ante-bellum South* (New York: Vintage Books, 1956) and Stanley M. Elkins' *Slavery: A Problem in American Institutional and Intellectual Life* (Chicago: University of Chicago Press, 1959) coincided with the more publicly demonstrative activities of the Civil Rights Movement. Furthermore, studies of the slave, slave resistance, and slave culture in the late 1960s and early 1970s were influenced not only by the Civil Rights Movement, but also by the Black Power, Black Nationalist, and Black Studies movements of the time. See Meier and Rudwick, *Black History and the Historical Profession, 1915–1980,* chapter 3.

13. George Rawick, *The American Slave: A Composite Autobiography,* Vol. 1, *From Sundown to Sunup: The Making of the Slave Community* (Westport, Conn.: Greenwood Publishing Co., 1972), pp. 14–28, 138–39.

14. Provision grounds were garden plots allocated by slaveowners to slaves for the slaves' own use in raising additional food, particularly table vegetables. The allocation of such plots was often a reward for work accomplished, or sometimes a vital means of sustaining nutritional health in the slave quarter.

15. A notable exception, among others, is the work of George P. Rawick, "Some Notes on a Social Analysis of Slavery: A Critical Assessment of the Slave Community," in Revisiting Blassingame's *The Slaves Community: The Scholars Respond,* ed. Al-Tony Gilmore (Westport, Conn.: Greenwood Publishing Co., 1978), pp. 17–26.

16. Additional works in the new generation of blackwomen slave historians include: Angela Davis, *Women, Race, and Class* (New York: Random House, 1981); Paula Giddings, *When and Where I Enter: The Impact of Black Women on Race and Sex in America* (New York: William Morrow & Co., 1984); Dorothy Sterling, *We Are Your Sisters; Black Women in the Nineteenth Century* (New York: W. W. Norton & Co., 1984); Marietta Morrissey, *Slave Women in the New World: Gender Stratification in the Caribbean* (Lawrence, Kans.: University of Kansas, 1989); *Black Women in United States History: From Colonial Times to the Present,* 16 vols., ed. Darlene Clark Hine, Elsa Barkley Brown, et. al. (Brooklyn, N.Y.: Carlson, 1993); *Discovering the Women in Slavery: Emancipating Perspectives on the American Past,* ed. Patricia Morton (Athens, Ga.: University of Georgia Press, 1996); and *More than Chattel: Black Women and Slavery in the*

Americas, ed. David Barry Gaspar and Darlene Clark Hine (Bloomington, Ind.: Indiana University Press, 1996).

17. White, *Ar'nt I a Woman? Female Slaves in the Plantation South* (New York: W. W. Norton & Co., 1985), p. 23.

18. Jacqueline Jones, *Labor of Love, Labor of Sorrow: Black Women, Work and the Family, from Slavery to the Present* (New York: Vintage Books, 1985), p. 14.

19. White, *Ar'nt I a Woman,* p. 137.

20. A growing body of evidence argues for the reclamation of historical, biblical, and hermeneutical perspectives for the development of Christianity in Africa and for the formation of an ancient Ethiopian canon. In biblical studies, for example, see Cain Hope Felder, *Troubling Biblical Waters: Race, Class, and Family* (Maryknoll, N.Y.: Orbis Books, 1990); Clarice J. Martin, "A Chamberlain's Journey and The Challenge of Interpretation for Liberation," *Semeia* 47 (1989), pp.105–35; and Charles B. Copher, "3,000 Years of Biblical Interpretation with Reference to Black Peoples," *Journal of the Interdenominational Theological Center* 30, no. 2 (Spring 1986): 225–46.

21. George P. Rawick, *The American Slave: A Composite Autobiography, Vol. 1: From Sundown to Sunup—The Making of the Black Community* (Westport, Conn.: Greenwood Press, 1972), p. 37.

22. Norman R. Yetman, ed., *Voices from Slavery: The Life of American Slaves—In the Words of 100 Men and Women Who Lived It and Many Years Later Talked About It* (New York: Holt, Rinehart, & Winston, 1970), p. 228.

23. For a discussion of a theory of reading as production, see J. Severino Croatto, *Biblical Hermeneutics: Toward a Theory of Reading as the Production of Meaning* (Maryknoll, N.Y.: Orbis Books, 1987).

24. Walter Harrelson, "Life, Faith, and the Emergence of Tradition," in *Tradition and Theology in the Old Testament,* ed. Douglas A. Knight (London: SPCK Press, 1977), pp. 11–30. Harrelson draws on the work of Douglas A. Knight and Josef Pieper.

25. Ibid., p. 18.

26. Ibid., pp. 14–15.

27. George P. Rawick, ed., *The American Slave: A Composite Autobiography,* 41 Vols. (Westport, Conn.: Greenwood Publishing Co., 1972), Supplement 2, vol. 4, p. 1,052.

28. James Mellon, ed., *Bullwhip Days: The Slaves Remember—An Oral History* (New York: Avon Books, 1988), p. 190.

29. See the works such as Gayraud S. Wilmore, *Black Religion and Black Radicalism: An Interpretation of the Religious History of Afro-American People* (3rd rev. ed. 1998); James H. Cone, *The Spirituals and the Blues* (reprint ed., 1992) and *God of the Oppressed* (1975); Lawrence N. Jones, "Black Christians in Antebellum America: The Quest for the Beloved Community," *The Journal of Black Thought,*

vol. 38, no. 1 (Summer 1987): pp. 12–19; and the authors of *Cut Loose Your Stammering Tongue: The Slave Narrative in Black Theology,* ed. Dwight N. Hopkins and George C. L. Cummings (1991); *A Troublin' in My Soul: Womanist Perspectives on Evil and Suffering,* ed. Emilie M. Townes (1993); *Embracing the Spirit: Womanist Perspectives on Hope, Salvation and Transformation,* ed. Emilie M. Townes (1997); and Riggins R. Earl, *Dark Symbols, Obscure Signs: God, Self, and Community in the Slave Mind* (1993).

30. Mechal Sobel, *Trabelin' On: The Slave Journey to an Afro-Baptist Faith* (Princeton, N.J.: Princeton University Press, 1988), p. 113.

31. Earl, *Dark Symbols, Obscure Signs,* p. 173.

32. Sarah Bradford, *Harriet Tubman: The Moses of Her People* (New York: Corinth Books, 1961), p. 30 as quoted in George C. L. Cummings, "The Spirit and Eschatology," in *Cut Loose Your Stammering Tongue: The Slave Narrative in Black Theology,* ed. Dwight N. Hopkins and George C. L. Cummings (Maryknoll, N.Y.: Orbis Books, 1991), p. 58.

33. Cone, *God of the Oppressed,* p. 57.

34. Dwight N. Hopkins, "Slave Theology in the Invisible Institution," in *Cut Loose Your Stammering Tongue,* p. 1.

35. Although not an exhaustive list, womanist theologians and ethicists utilizing the slave narrative corpus include Katie G. Cannon, Jacqueline D. Carr-Hamilton, Shawn Copeland, Cheryl Kirk-Duggan, Theresa Frye, Jacquelyn Grant, Marcia Y. Riggs, and Delores S. Williams.

36. Jacquelyn Grant, *White Women's Christ and Black Women's Jesus: Feminist Christology and Womanist Response* (Atlanta: Scholars Press, 1989), p. 211–18.

37. Katie G. Cannon, "The Emergence of Black Feminist Consciousness," in *Feminist Interpretation of the Bible,* ed. Letty M. Russell (Philadelphia: Westminster Press, 1985), p. 40.

38. Katie G. Cannon, "Surviving the Blight," in *Inheriting Our Mothers' Gardens: Feminist Theology in Third World Perspective,* ed. Letty M. Russell, et. al., (Philadelphia: Westminster Press, 1988), pp. 75–90.

39. Williams, *Sisters in the Wilderness,* pp. 199–203.

40. Katie G. Cannon, *Black Womanist Ethics* (Atlanta, Ga.: Scholars Press, 1988), pp. 31–4.

41. Katie G. Cannon, "Slave Ideology and Biblical Interpretation," *Semeia* 47 (1989), pp. 9–23.

42. Cannon, *Black Womanist Ethics,* pp. 125–44.

43. Cheryl J. Sanders, "Roundtable Discussion: Christian Ethics and Theology in Womanist Perspective: A Final Rejoinder," in *The Journal of Feminist Studies in Religion* vol. 5, no. 2 (1989): pp. 83–91.

44. Hopkins and Cummings, *Cut Loose Your Stammering Tongue,* p. xvi.

45. Ibid., p. xviii.

Chapter 2: Tools of the Trade

1. For discussion of the slave trade origin and development in the New World, see Eugene D. Genovese, *The Political Economy of Slavery: Studies in the Economy and Society of the Slave South,* 2nd ed. (Middletown, Conn.: Wesleyan University Press, 1989), and Robert William Fogel and Stanley L. Engerman, *Time on the Cross: The Economics of American Negro Slavery,* rev. ed. (New York: W. W. Norton & Co., 1989).

2. Fogel and Engerman, *Time On The Cross,* p. 29.

3. Stanley Elkins, *Slavery* (Chicago: University of Chicago, 1976), p. 43.

4. Ibid., p. 44, note 24.

5. David Bertelson, *The Lazy South* (New York: Oxford University Press, 1967), p. 19.

6. For further discussion of the relation between free labor, indentured servitude, and the institutionalization of slavery, see Winthrop D. Jordan, *White over Black: American Attitudes toward the Negro, 1550–1812,* (Chapel Hill: University of North Carolina Press, 1968; New York: W. W. Norton Co., 1977), pt.1, chap. 2.

7. Ibid., p. 66.

8. David Brion Davis, "Slavery and the Meaning of America," reprint 1966, in *Myth and Southern History, Vol. 1: The Old South,* 2nd. ed., ed. Patrick Gerster and Nicholas Cords (Urbana, Ill.: University of Illinois Press, 1989), pp. 31–32.

9. McGary and Larson, *Slavery,* p. 6, as quoted from William E. Moore, *American Negro Slavery and Abolition* (New York: Third World Press, 1971), p. 9.

10. Lerone Bennett, Jr., *The Shaping of Black America: The Struggles and Triumphs of African Americans, 1619 to the 1990s* (Chicago: Johnson Publishing Co., 1969; New York: Penguin Books, 1993), 66; Winthrop D. Jordan, *White over Black,* p. 92.

11. Jordan, *White over Black,* p. 78.

12. Ibid., p. 125.

13. Peter J. Paris, *The Social Teachings of the Black Churches* (Philadelphia: Fortress Press, 1985), p. 60.

14. Ibid., pp. 57–61.

15. Dona Marimba Richards, *Let the Circle Be Unbroken: Implications of African Spirituality in the Diaspora* (Trenton: Red Sea Press, 1989), p. 4.

16. I am indebted to the work of several scholars for influencing my thinking in this area: two scholars with whom I studied at Temple University, Leonard Barrett, author of *Soul–Force: African Heritage in Afro-American Religion* (Garden City, N.J.: Anchor Press/Doubleday & Co., 1974) and Karen McCarthy Brown, author of several essays and *Mama Lola: A Vodou Priestess in Brooklyn,* (Berkeley, Calif.: University of California Press, 1991); Roger Bastide, *African Civiliza-*

tions in the New World, trans. Peter Green (London: C. Hurst & Co., 1966) and *The African Religions of Brazil: Toward a Sociology of the Interpenetration of Civilizations* (Baltimore: Johns Hopkins University Press, 1987); Albert J. Raboteau, *Slave Religion: The Invisible Institution in the Antebellum South* (New York: Oxford University Press, 1978); and Sydney Mintz and Richard Price, *The Birth of African American Culture: An Anthropological Perspective* ([Philadelphia: Institute for the Study of Human Issues, 1976]; Boston: Beacon Press, 1992).

17. By "theo-ethical tools" I mean presuppositions, methods, and strategies that inform the development of systematic, normative social ethic grounded in the biblical and theological traditions of Christian faith.

18. Clifford Geertz, *The Interpretation of Cultures* (New York: Basic Books, 1973), p. 13.

19. Rawick, *From Sundown to Sunup,* p. 86.

20. Ibid., p. 87.

21. Sterling Stuckey, *Slave Culture, Nationalist Theory and the Foundations of Black America* (New York: Oxford University Press, 1987), p. 1.

22. Molefi Kete Asante and Kariamu Welsh Asante, eds. *African Culture: The Rhythms of Unity* (Westport, Conn.: Greenwood Press, 1985), pp. ix–x.

23. In using the term *African common orientations,* I follow the suggestion of Lawrence Levine and refrain from using the term *African survivals* or *African retentions.* Levine notes that the latter two terms prejudice the issue prior to its discussion, and posits such elements as mere vestiges or quaint reminders of an exotic culture enough alive to make it picturesquely different but not substantial. See Lawrence Levine, *Black Culture and Black Consciousness: Afro-American Folk Thought from Slavery to Freedom* (Oxford: Oxford University Press, 1977), pp. 3–4, and George Brandon, "Sacrifical Practices in Santeria, An Afro-Cuban Religion in the United States," *in Africanisms in American Culture,* ed. Joseph E. Holloway (Bloomington, Ind.: Indiana University Press, 1990), p. 143.

24. Karen McCarthy Brown, "Systematic Remembering, Systematic Forgetting: Ogou in Haiti," in *Africa's Ogun: Old World and New,* ed. by Sandra T. Barnes (Bloomington, Ind.: Indiana University Press, 1989), p. 66.

25. James Mellon, ed. *Bullwhip Days: The Slaves Remember: An Oral History* (New York: Avon Books, 1988), p. 192.

26. Will Coleman, "Coming Through 'Ligion: Metaphor in Non-and-Christian Experiences with the Spirit in African American Slave Narratives," in *Cut Loose Your Stammering Tongue: Black Theology in the Slave Narratives,* p. 68.

27. Charles Colcock Jones, *The Religious Instruction of the Negroes in the United States* (Savannah, Ga., 1842), p. 114, as quoted in Albert J. Raboteau, *Slave Religion,* p. 117.

28. Mellon, ed., *Bullwhip Days,* p. 121; also see Stuckey, *Slave Culture,* pp. 91–92.

29. Ibid., p. 190.

30. Peter J. Paris, *The Spirituality of African Peoples: The Search for a Common Moral Discourse* (Minneapolis: Fortress Press, 1995), p. 25.

31. Barrett, *Soul Force,* p. 27.

32. Paris, *The Spirituality of African Peoples,* p. 22.

33. Alice Walker, *In Search of Our Mothers' Gardens: A Womanist Prose* (New York: Harcourt Brace Jovanovich, 1983), xi–xii.

34. See, for example, Jacquelyn Grant, *White Women's Christ and Black Women's Jesus: Feminist Christology and Womanist Response* (Atlanta: Scholars Press, 1989) and Delores S. Williams, *Sisters in the Wilderness: The Challenge of Womanist God-Talk* (Maryknoll, N.Y.: Orbis, 1993).

35. Kate G. Cannon, "The Emergence of Black Feminist Consciousness," in *Feminist Interpretation of the Bible,* ed. Letty M. Russell (Philadelphia: Westminster Press, 1985), and Delores Williams, *Sisters in the Wilderness,* op. cit.

36. Cheryl J. Sanders, "Roundtable Discussion: Christian Ethics and Theology in Womanist Perspective: A Final Rejoinder" in *The Journal of Feminist Studies in Religion,* vol. 5, no. 2 (1989): p. 111.

37. Katie G. Cannon, *Black Womanist Ethics,* p. 4.

38. Ibid., p. 2.

39. Ibid., pp. 2–3.

40. Katie G. Cannon, *Katie's Canon: Womanism and the Soul of the Black Community* (New York: Continuum Publishing Co., 1995), pp. 136–41.

41. Albert J. Raboteau, *Slave Religion: The Invisible Institution in the Antebellum South* (New York: Oxford University Press, 1978), p. 7; Levine, *Black Culture and Black Consciousness,* pp. 3–4.

42. Pierre Bourdieu, *In Other Words: Toward a Reflexive Sociology* (Stanford, Ca.: Stanford University Press, 1990), p. 126.

43. Pierre Bourdieu, *Outline of a Theory of Practice,* trans. Richard Nice (Cambridge: Cambridge University Press, 1977; reprint, 1991), p. 72. Objective structures and relations are systems independent of individual consciousness and will. Generally, they are systems, institutional apparatus, and parts of society, independent and yet related, which more or less organize it.

44. Loic J. D. Wacquant, "Toward a Reflexive Sociology: A Workshop with Pierre Bourdieu," *Sociological Theory,* vol. 7, no. 1 (Spring 1989): p. 37ff.

45. John B. Thompson, "Editor's Introduction," *Language and Symbolic Power,* by Pierre Bourdieu (Cambridge, Mass.: Harvard University Press, 1991), p. 16.

46. Drew Gilpin Faust, *James Henry Hammond and the Old South: A Design for Mastery* (Baton Rouge, La.: Louisiana State University Press, 1982), p. 74.

47. Bourdieu, *In Other Words,* pp. 62–63.

48. Ibid., p. 63.

49. White, *Ar'nt I a Woman,* p. 129.

50. Bourdieu, *In Other Words,* p. 10.

51. Beverly W. Harrison, *Making the Connections: Essays in Feminist Social Ethics,* ed. Carol S. Robb (Boston: Beacon Press, 1985), p. 13.

52. Hiram Mattison, *Louisa Picquet, the Octoroon: or A Tale of Southern Slave Life,* 1861. Reprinted in *Collected Black Women's Narratives,* The Schomburg Library of Nineteenth-Century Black Women Writers, ed. Henry Louis Gates, Jr. (New York: Oxford University Press, 1988), p. 5.

53. Barbara Welter, "The Cult of True Womanhood, 1820–1860," in *Dimity Convictions: The American Woman in the Nineteenth Century* (Columbus, Ohio: University of Ohio, 1976), pp. 21–41 as quoted in Hazel V. Carby, *Reconstructing Womanhood: The Emergence of the Afro-American Woman Novelist* (New York: Oxford University Press, 1987), pp. 20–39. Also see Catherine Clinton, *The Plantation Mistress: Woman's World in the Old South* (New York: Pantheon Books, 1982), chap. 1.

54. Jacobs, *Incidents,* p. 13; also see, Mattison, *Louisa Picquet, Octoroon,* p. 6 for a similar incident.

55. K. Sue Jewell, *From Mammy to Miss America and Beyond: Cultural Images and the Shaping of U.S. Social Policy* (London: Routledge & Kegan Paul, 1993), p. 60.

56. Pierre Bourdieu, *Distinction: A Social Critique of the Judgement of Taste* (London: Routledge & Kegan Paul, 1984), chap. 7 and conclusion.

57. *FWPSN,* Oklahoma, p. 172, as quoted in Rawick, *From Sundown to Sunup,* p. 68.

58. Earl, Jr., *Dark Symbols, Obscure Signs,* p. 47.

59. R. M. Henry, "The Police Control of the Slave in South Carolina," (Diss., Vanderbilt University, 1914), pp. 182–183, as cited in Theodore Branter Wilson, *The Black Codes of the South* (University, Ala.: University of Alabama Press, 1965), p. 27.

60. Ralph B. Sanders, "The Free Negro in Ante-Bellum Georgia," *North Carolina Historical Review,* IX (July 1932), p. 262, as cited in Wilson, *Black Codes,* p. 41. Note the economic suppression directed at blacks intended in this law as well as restriction of bodily freedom and expression.

61. Bourdieu, *In Other Words,* p. 12.

62. Bourdieu, *Outline,* p. 72.

63. Bourdieu, *Logic of Practice,* pp. 67–70.

64. Thompson, "Editor's Introduction," in Bourdieu, *Language and Symbolic Power,* p. 12.

65. Gladys-Marie Frye, *Stitches from the Soul: Slave Quilts from the Ante-Bellum South,* (New York: E. P. Dutton, 1990), p. 15, as quoted in Cuesta Benberry, *Always There: The African American Presence in American Quilts* (Louisville, Ky.: The Kentucky Quilt Project, Inc., Museum of History and Science, 1992), p. 27.

66. Bourdieu, *Logic of Practice,* p. 53.

67. Bourdieu, *Logic of Practice,* p. 126.

68. Faust, *James Henry Hammond,* p. 74.

69. Hammond Plantation Diary, December 15, 16, 1831; May 11, 1832, as quoted in Faust, *James Henry Hammond,* p. 74.

70. Jacobs, *Incidents,* pp. 63–67.

71. Ibid., p. 19.

72. Ibid., p. 19.

73. "All God's chillun got shoes" is a stanza from the slave spiritual, "All God's Chillun Got Wings." Ethnomusicologist John Lovell writes, "Some garments express the creative urge . . . They transform the slave from the ordinary worker and being some people (including masters, overseers, and auctioneers) consider him . . . All he needs is the chance." John Lovell, Jr., *Black Song: The Forge and the Flame* (New York: MacMillan Publishing Co., 1972), p. 284.

74. James C. Scott, *Domination and the Arts of Resistance: Hidden Transcripts* (New Haven, Conn.: Yale University Press, 1990), pp. 4–5.

75. Ibid., p. 2.

76. Ibid, p. xii. Further, I recognize that Scott's contribution is helpful for my purposes, while not original. Much of the established scholarship on North American slavery uses prior anthropological data and research to theorize issues of enslaved volition, African orientations, and power relations. See the comments of Michael A. Gomez, *Exchanging Our Country Masks: The Transformation of African Identities in the Colonial and Antebellum South* (Chapel Hill, N.C.: University of North Carolina Press, 1998), pp. 8–9, and note 18, chap. 1.

77. Ibid., p. 203.

78. White, *Ar'nt I a Woman,* p. 116.

79. Rawick, *Arkansas and Missouri Narratives,* vol. 11, pt. 7, p. 53.

80. Ibid., p. 14.

81. Rawick, *Texas Narratives,* vol. 4, pt. 2, p. 163.

82. Ibid., p. 77. Cf. Bourdieu, *Distinction,* p. 471.

83. Scott, *Domination and the Arts of Resistance,* pp. 70–76.

84. Rawick, *Arkansas and Missouri Narratives,* vol. 11, pt. 8, p. 284.

85. Scott, *Domination and the Arts of Resistance,* p. 80.

86. Raboteau, *Slave Religion,* p. 285.

87. Levine, *Black Culture,* pp. 49–51.

88. Ibid., p. 51.

89. Ibid., p. 81.

90. See The Book of Exodus, esp. chapters 1–20; Matthew 20:1–20; Luke 16:19–31; and Acts 5:1–11.

91. For discussion of the Christian utopian religious understanding and African religious influence on Denmark Vesey and Nat Turner, see Gayraud S. Wilmore, *Black Religion and Black Radicalism,* pp. 57–59, 64–69;and Sterling Stuckey, *Slave Culture,* pp. 43–50.

Chapter 3: By Perseverance and Unwearied Industry

1. Gerald Jaynes, "Plantation Factories and the Slave Work Ethic," in *The Slave's Narrative,* ed. Charles T. Davis and Henry Louis Gates, Jr. (New York: Oxford University Press, 1985), p. 103.

2. Donald G. Mathews, *Religion in the Old South* (Chicago: University of Chicago Press, 1977) p. 1.

3. Ibid., p. 15.

4. Elizabeth Fox-Genovese and Eugene Genovese, "The Divine Sanction of Social Order: Religious Foundations of the Southern Slaveholders' World View," in *The Journal of the American Academy of Religion,* vol. LV, no. 2 (summer 1987): p. 211.

5. Mathews, *Religion in the Old South,* p. 173.

6. *Christian Advocate and Journal,* February 12, 1836, p. 98 as quoted in Donald G. Mathews, *Slavery and Methodism: A Chapter in American Morality* (Princeton, N.J.: Princeton University Press, 1965), p. 78.

7. Ibid., p. 87.

8. Slave historians who debate a slave work ethic include Robert William Fogel and Stanley L. Engerman, *Time on the Cross,* p. 147ff; Eugene D. Genovese, *Roll, Jordan Roll,* pp. 286ff; Herbert Gutman and Richard Sutch, "Sambo Makes Good, or Were Slaves Imbued with the Protestant Work Ethic," in *Reckoning with Slavery: A Critical Study in the Quantitative History of American Negro Slavery,* ed. Paul A. David, et. al., (New York: Oxford University Press, 1976), p. 69ff; Gerald Jaynes, "Plantation Factories and the Slave Work Ethic," pp. 98–112; Charles Joyner, *Down by the Riverside: A South Carolina Slave Community* (Urbana, Ill.: University of Illinois Press,1984), pp. 50–57; and George P. Rawick, ed., *From Sundown to Sunup: The Making of the Black Community,* vol. 1, *The American Slave: A Composite Autobiography* (Westport, Conn.: Greenwood Publishing Co., 1972) pp. 138–140. The-ologians and ethicists who discuss the issue include Dwight Hopkins, *Shoes That Fit Our Feet: Sources for a Constructive Black Theology* (Maryknoll, N.Y.: Orbis Books, 1993), p. 136ff; Riggins Earl, *Dark Symbols, Obscure Signs: God, Self, and Community in the Slave Mind* (Maryknoll, N.Y.: Orbis Books, 1993), pp.149–152.

9. Cheryl J. Sanders, "Liberation Ethics in the Ex-Slave Interviews" in *Cut Loose Your Stammering Tongue: The Slave Narrative in Black Theology* (Maryknoll, N.Y.: Orbis Books, 1991), pp. 103–36.

10. George P. Rawick, ed., *The American Slave: A Composite Autobiography,* 41 Vols. (Westport, Conn.: Greenwood Publishing Co., 1972), *Texas Narratives,* vol. 4, pt. 1, p. 44.

11. Elizabeth, *The Memoir of Old Elizabeth, a Coloured Woman* (Philadelphia: Collins Printer, 1863). Reprinted in *Six Women's Slave Narratives,* The Schomburg Library of Nineteenth-Century Black Women Writers, ed. Henry Louis Gates, Jr. (New York: Oxford University Press, 1988), p. 4.

12. Elizabeth Kleckley, *Behind the Scenes, or Thirty Years a Slave and Four Years in the White House.* Reprinted by The Schomburg Library of Nineteenth-Century Black Women Writers, ed. Henry Louis Gates, Jr. (New York: Oxford University Press, 1988), p. xii.

13. Ibid., p. xii.

14. Sojourner Truth, *The Narrative of Sojourner Truth.* [1850 edition as dictated to Olive Gilbert]; ed. with introduction by Margaret Washington (New York: Vintage Books, 1993), p. 11.

15. Ibid., p. 31.

16. Harriet Jacobs, *Incidents in the Life of a Slave Girl. Written by Herself,* ed. L. Maria Child (1861; reprint, with an introduction by Jean Fagan Yellin, Cambridge: Harvard University Press, 1987), pp. 90–91.

17. Sterling Stuckey, *Slave Culture,* pp. 12–14.

18. Rawick, *Texas Narratives,* vol. 5, pt. 3, p. 213.

19. Rawick., *South Carolina Narratives,* vol . 2 , pt. 2 , p. 184.

20. Rawick, *Arkansas and Missouri Narratives,* vol. 11, pt. 7, p. 182.

21. *Aunt Sally, or The Cross the Way of Freedom: A Narrative of the Slave-Life and Purchase of the Mother of Rev. Isaac Williams* [Cincinnati: American Reform Tract and Book Society, 1858]. (Reprinted, Miami: Mnemosyne Publishing Co., 1969), p. 27.

22. Jacobs, *Incidents,* p.7.

23. Ibid., p. 11, 17. The phrase "by perseverance and unwearied industry" serves as the title for this chapter because of its depiction of the labor of enslaved and ex-enslaved women, and the moral agency and quality of their work.

24. Ibid., p. 115.

25. Ibid., pp. 11–12.

26. Ibid., p. 54.

27. Ibid., p. 99ff.

28. Joanne M. Braxton, *Black Women Writing Autobiography: A Tradition within a Tradition* (Philadelphia: Temple University Press, 1989), p. 20.

29. Rawick, *South Carolina Narratives,* vol. 2, pt. 1, p. 173.

30. Angela Davis, "Reflections on the Black Woman's Role in the Community of Slaves," *The Black Scholar* 3 (December 1971): pp. 3–15.

31. Rawick, *Texas Narratives,* Supplement, series 2, vol. 6, pt. 5, p. 1943.

32. Kleckley, *Behind the Scenes,* pp. 38–39.

33. Hiram Mattison, *Louisa Picquet, the Octoroon: Or the Inside Views of Southern Domestic Life,* 1861. Reprinted in *Collected Black Women's*

Narratives, The Schomburg Library of Nineteenth-Century Black Women Writers, ed. Henry Louis Gates, Jr. (New York: Oxford University Press, 1988), p. 19.

34. Kleckley, *Behind the Scenes,* pp. 38–39.

35. Ibid., p. 39.

36. Jacobs, *Incidents,* p. 189.

37. Mattison, *Louisa Picquet,* p. 19.

38. Carby, *Reconstructing Womanhood,* pp. 23–25.

39. Ibid., p. 27.

40. Jacobs, *Incidents,* p. 55.

41. Ibid., p. 77.

42. Catherine Clinton, *The Plantation Mistress: Women's World in the Old South* (New York: Pantheon Books, 1982), p. 201.

43. White, *Ar'nt I a Woman,* p. 47.

44. Ibid., pp. 47 and 49.

45. Jacobs, *Incidents,* p. 144.

46. Ibid., p. 143.

47. Ibid., p. 31.

48. Elizabeth Fox-Genovese, *Within the Plantation Household: Black and White Women of the Old South,* (Chapel Hill, N.C.: University of North Carolina Press, 1988), p. 291.

49. Ibid., p. 291.

50. Jacobs, *Incidents,* p. 144.

51. Katie G. Cannon, "Resources for a Constructive Womanist Ethics," Religion Course 906, Temple University, 1993.

52. Delores S. Williams, *Sisters in the Wilderness: The Challenge of Womanist God-Talk* (Maryknoll, N.Y.: Orbis Books, 1993), p. 50.

53. See Jacobs, *Incidents,* chap. 5–6, and Mattison, *Louisa Picquet,* pp. 12–13.

54. Cannon, "Resources for a Constructive Womanist Ethics," Religion Course 906, 1993.

55. Jacobs, *Incidents,* p. 17.

56. Ibid., p. 1.

57. Lucy A. Delaney, *From the Darkness Cometh the Light, or Struggles for Freedom* [St. Louis: J. T. Smith Publishing House, (c. 1891)]. Reprinted in *Six Women's Slave Narratives,* The Schomburg Library of Nineteenth-Century Black Women Writers, ed. Henry Louis Gates, Jr. (New York: Oxford University Press, 1988), pp. 52–53.

58. Kleckely, *Behind the Scenes,* pp. 46–47; 54–55.

59. *Aunt Sally, or the Cross the Way of Freedom,* pp. 92–98.

60. *Douglass' Monthly,* vol. 1, no. 8, January 1859.

61. Ibid., vol. 1, no. 8, January 1859.

62. Davis, "Reflection on the Black Woman's Role in the Community of Slaves," p. 7.

63. Rawick, *Arkansas and Missouri Narratives,* vol. 11, pt. 7, p. 3.

64. Octavia V. Rogers Albert, *The House of Bondage: Or Aunt Charlotte Brooks and Other Slaves* [1890]. Reprinted in The Schomburg Library of Nineteenth-Century Black Women Writers, ed. by Henry Louis Gates, Jr. (New York: Oxford University Press, 1988), p. 20.

65. Deborah Gray White, *Ar'nt I a Woman,* p. 74.

66. Rawick, *South Carolina Narratives,* vol. 2, pt. 1, p. 100.

67. Truth, *The Narrative of Sojourner Truth,* p. 3.

68. Rawick, *South Carolina Narratives,* vol. 3, pt. 4, p. 219.

69. Benjamin Ray, *African Religions: Symbols, Ritual, and Community* (Englewood Cliffs, N.J.: Prentice-Hall, 1976), pp. 150–53.

70. Mattison, *Louisa Picquet,* p. 17.

71. Shawn Copeland, "Wading through Many Sorrows: Toward a Theology of Suffering in a Womanist Perspective," in *A Troubling in My Soul: Womanist Perspectives on Evil and Suffering,* ed. Emilie M. Townes (Maryknoll, N.Y.: Orbis Books, 1993), p. 123.

72. Williams, *Sisters in the Wilderness,* p. 166. See chapter 6 for a discussion of suffering and Christological atonement from a womanist perspective.

73. Jacobs, *Incidents,* pp. 68–69.

Chapter 4: Whose Work Ethic?

1. For a discussion of the notion of "labor" as the production of life necessities and "work" as "worldliness," see Hannah Arendt, *The Human Condition* (Chicago: University of Chicago Press, 1958), pp. 7, 45–6, and 136ff.

2. Jürgen Moltmann, *On Human Dignity: Political Theology and Ethics* (Philadelphia: Fortress Press, 1984), p. 39.

3. *Ibid.,* p. 40.

4. For this first framework, see Alan Richardson, *The Biblical Doctrine of Work,* Ecumenical Biblical Studies No. 1, (London: SCM Press, 1952), p. 13.

5. Early examples include James H. Cone, *God of the Oppressed,* op.cit., p. 11, Phyllis Trible, "Depatriarchalizing in Biblical Interpretation," *Journal of the American Academy of Religion* 41 (1973): pp. 34ff, and Dorothee Söelle with Shirley A. Cloyes, *To Love and to Work: A Theology of Creation* (Philadelphia: Fortress Press, 1984), p. 7.

6. Renita J. Weems, "Reading Her Way through the Struggle: African American Women and the Bible," in *Stony the Road We Trod: African American Biblical Interpretation,* ed. Cain Hope Felder (Minneapolis: Fortress Press, 1991), pp. 60–69.

7. Ibid., p. 59.

8. Ibid., p. 58–59.

9. For a similar theo-ethical reflection, but on the theme of black mothers, surrogacy, and the biblical story of Hagar, see Delores S. Williams, *Sisters in the Wilderness,* op. cit.

10. Terence E. Freitheim, *Exodus: Interpretation—a Bible Commentary for Teaching and Preaching* (Louisville, Ky.: John Knox Press, 1991), p. 26.

11. Ibid., p. 35.

12. Although the text is inconclusive about whether the women were Hebrew women or Egyptian women serving the Hebrew community, clearly one of the central features of the midwives' action is its solidarity with Israelite women. The actual identity of these women cannot be resolved by biblical scholarship.

13. J. Cheryl Exum, "You Shall Let Every Daughter Live: A Study of Exodus 1:8–2:10," *Semeia* 28, (1983), p. 72.

14. The reader should note that Exum has twice revisited her thesis in the above cited essay in "Second Thoughts about Secondary Characters: Women in Exodus 1:8–2:10," in *A Feminist Companion to Exodus to Deuteronomy,* ed. Athalya Brenner (Sheffield: Sheffield Academic Press, 1994), pp. 75–87, and *Plotted, Shot, and Painted: Cultural Representations of Biblical Women* (Sheffield: Sheffield Academic Press, 1996), chap. 4. Her self-criticism concerns the marginality of women in the full Exodus narrative when chapters 1–2 focus so positively on women, and the role the early focus has for a basically androcentric and patriachal text whose central character is Moses, the male hero. Methodologically, Exum also has shifted to deconstruction of reading texts along with feminist literary criticism of texts. I note her concern and attempt to address it somewhat through a "blackwoman's" reading. It is, however, a problem for which neither Exum nor I have a solution.

15. Ibid., p. 73.

16. Ibid., p. 73.

17. Freitheim, *Exodus,* p. 36.

18. Rawick, *Arkansas Narratives,* vol. 11, pt. 7, p 21.

19. White, *Ar'nt I a Woman,* p.112.

20. Söelle, *To Work and to Love,* p.12.

21. Martin Luther, *Luther's Works,* vol. 44, ed. Helmut Lehmann (Philadelphia: Fortress Press, 1966), pp. 129–30.

22. Moltmann, *On Human Dignity,* p. 47.

23. John Calvin, *Institutes of the Christian Religion,* vol. 1., ed. John T. McNeill, *The Library of Christian Classics,* vol. XX (Philadelphia: Westminster Press, 1955), p. 725.

24. Ibid., p. 695.

25. Jane Dempsey Douglass, *Women, Freedom, and Calvin* (Philadelphia: Westminster Press, 1985), pp. 114–15.

26. John T. McNeill, *The History and Character of Calvinism* (New York: Oxford University Press, 1967), p. 221.

27. E. William Monter, *Calvin's Geneva* (New York: John Wiley & Sons, 1967), p. 4.

28. McNeill, *The History and Character of Calvinism,* p. 185.

29. Abel Athouguia Alves, "The Christian Social Organism and Social Welfare: The Case of Vives, Calvin, and Loyola," *Sixteenth Century Journal* xx, no. 1 (1989): p. 8.

30. *Ibid.*, p. 9.

31. For further discussion of this interpretation of Calvin's theology, see Barbara Hilkert Andolsen, *Good Work at the Video Display Terminal—A Feminist Ethical Analysis of Clerical Work* (Knoxville, Tenn.: University of Tennessee Press, 1989), pp. 99–100.

32. Luther, *Luther's Works,* vol. 44, pp. 189–90.

33. Robert Wuthnow, *Poor Richard's Principle: Recovering the American Dream through the Moral Dimension of Work, Business, and Money* (Princeton. N.J.: Princeton University Press, 1996), p. 59.

34. Alves, "The Christian Social Organism and Social Welfare," pp. 12–13.

35. *Ibid.*, p. 19.

36. Andolsen, *Good Work at the Video Display,* pp. 97, 102.

37. Calvin, *The Institutes,* vol. 1, p. 723.

38. Richard Baxter as quoted in Winthrop S. Hudson, "Puritanism and the Spirit of Capitalism," *Church History,* 18, no. 12 (1949). For the contestable scholarly arguments about the relationship of Calvinism to capitalism, see Max Weber, *The Protestant Ethic and the Spirit of Capitalism* (New York: Charles Scribner's Sons, 1958) and R. H. Tawney, *Religion and the Rise of Capitalism* (New York: Harcourt, Brace, and Co., 1926).

39. Stephen Innes, *Creating the Commonwealth: The Economic Culture of Puritan New England* (New York: W. W. Norton & Co., 1995), pp. 111–12.

40. *Ibid.*, p. 112.

41. Mechal Sobel, *The World They Made Together: Black and White Values in Eighteenth-Century Virginia* (Princeton, N.J.: Princeton University Press, 1987), p. 3, asserts that by the eighteenth century, Virginia was the largest, most populous colony, and the "home for a significant number of emigrants to virtually all the later [southern] colonies."

42. *Ibid.,* chap. 1.

43. Daniel T. Rodgers, *The Work Ethic in Industrial America, 1850–1920* (Chicago: University of Chicago Press, 1978), p. 12.

44. James B. Gilbert, *Work without Salvation: America's Intellectual and Industrial Alienation, 1880–1910* (Baltimore: Johns Hopkins University Press, 1977), p. ix.

45. Rodgers, *The Work Ethic in Industrial America,* chap. 1.

46. Gilbert, *Work without Salvation,* pp.viii–ix.

47. *Ibid.,* p. ix.

48. See Ernst Troeltsch, *The Social Teachings of the Christian Churches,* vol. 2 [1931], (Chicago: University of Chicago Press, reprint 1981), pp. 644–46, "Calvinism and Capitalism."

49. C. Vann Woodward, "The Southern Ethic in a Puritan World," in *Myth and Southern History,* vol. 1, 2nd ed., ed. Patrick Gerster and Nicholas Cords (Urbana, Ill.: University of Illinois Press, 1974, 1989), p. 51.

50. W. J. Cash, *The Mind of the South* (New York, 1941) as quoted by Woodward, "The Southern Ethic in a Puritan World," p. 43.

51. Eugene D. Genoves, *The Political Economy of Slavery: Studies in the Economy and Society of the Slave South,* 2nd. ed, (Middletown, Conn.: Wesleyan University Press, 1989), p. 28.

52. Katie G. Cannon, *Black Womanist Ethics* (Atlanta: Scholars Press, 1988), p. 3.

53. Rodgers, *The Work Ethic in Industrial America,* p. 7.

54. I am indebted to Dr. Aminah Beverly McCloud for the notions of enforced dependency and other corollary ideas regarding work. Our conversations in 1994–95 at the Annual Meetings of the American Academy of Religion, and a reading of her unpublished manuscript, "A Response to John C. Raines and Donna C. Day-Lower," *Modern Work and Human Meaning* (Philadelphia: Westminster Press, 1986) have been invaluable.

55. Jacobs, *Incidents,* p. 10.

56. William Harris, "Work and the Family in Black Atlanta," in *Black Women in United States History,* vol. II, ed. Darlene Clark Hine (Brooklyn, N.Y.: Carlson Publishing Co., 1990), p. 319.

57. *Aunt Sally or the Cross the Way of Freedom: A Narrative of the Life and Purchase of the Mother of Rev. Isaac Williams of Detroit, Michigan* [Cincinnati. American Reform Tract and Book Society, 1858], reprint (Miami: Mnemosyne Publishing Co., 1969), pp. 97–98.

58. C. Vann Woodward, "The Southern Ethic in a Puritan World," p. 57.

59. Ibid., pp. 57–58.

60. Harold Courlander, *Negro Folk Music, U.S.A.* (New York: Columbia University Press, 1963), p.117, as quoted in Sterling Stuckey, "Through the Prism of Folklore," *The Massachusetts Review* 9 (1968): pp. 417–37.

61. Elizabeth Kleckley, *Behind the Scenes,* p. 28.

Conclusion

1. Julianne Malveaux, "Section Introduction to Employment Issues," in *Slipping through the Cracks: The Status of Black Women,* eds. Margaret C. Simms and Julianne Malveaux (New Brunswick, N.J.: Transaction Publishers, 1986), p. 9.

2. Julianne Malveaux, "Section Introduction to Employment Issues," p. 8.

3. The first Executive Order barring racial employment discrimination in the federal government and by war industries was issued by President Franklin Roosevelt, as a move to forestall plans for a march on

Washington, D.C., called by A. Phillip Randolph, the president of the Brotherhood of Sleeping Car Porters. A second Executive Order by President Harry Truman desegregated the U.S. Armed Forces after World War II.

4. Jacqueline Jones, *American Work: Four Centuries of Black and White Labor* (New York: W. W. Norton & Co., 1998), p. 13.

5. U.S. Department of Labor, Bureau of Labor Statistics, *Report on Futurework: Trends and Challenges for Work in the 21st Century* [cited November 15, 1999]. Available from http://www.dol.gov/dol/asp/public/future/report/chapter1/main2.htm#5b.

6. U.S. Department of Labor, Bureau of Labor Statistics, *History of Federal Minimum Wage Rates Under the Fair Labor Standards Act, 1938–1996,* August 1999 [cited November 6, 1999]. Available from http://www.dol.gov/dol/esa/public/minwage/chart.htm.

7. U.S. Department of Labor, *Report on Futurework,* op. cit., chap. 2. http://www.dol.gov/dol/asp/public/futurework/report.htm.

8. Traci C. West, "Generating a Christian Ethical Approach to 'Welfare Reform,' " in *Shaping the Values That Shape Us: A National Consultation on Welfare Reform* (New York: The National Council of Churches of Christ in the U.S.A., 1998), p. 41.

9. Ibid., p. 42.

10. Mark Greenberg, "Two Years After: What Do We Know about How the Personal Responsibility and Work Opportunity Reconciliation Act Is Affecting Families?," in *Shaping the Values That Shape Us,* op. cit., p. 9.

11. LynNell Hancock, "Consultation on Welfare Reform and the Media," in *Shaping the Values That Shape Us,* op. cit., p. 32.

12. Jacobs, *Incidents,* p. 77.

13. My thinking along these lines has very much been influenced by the religious social ethics of Beverly Harrison. For further discussion of these issues, see Harrison's essay, "The Role of Social Theory in Religious Social Ethics," in Beverly W. Harrison, *Making the Connections,* pp. 54–82.

14. Jacobs, *Incidents,* p. xxxiii.

15. Nicola Pine, "Labor Exploitation in U.S. Prisons: A New Slave Labor," in *Women Against Military Madness Newsletter,* vol. 15, no. 4 (May 1997): p. 2.

16. *Ibid.,* p. 1.

17. Angela Davis, *The Angela Davis Reader,* ed. by Joy James (Malden, Mass.: Blackwell Publishers, 1998), p. 64, quoting from Marc Mauer, *Young Black Americans and the Criminal Justice System: Five Years Later* (Washington, D.C: The Sentencing Project, October 1995).

18. *Ibid.,* pp. 67–68.

19. McCloud, unpublished paper on "A Response to Modern Work and Human Meaning," p. 10.

20. Octavia V. Rogers Albert, *The House of Bondage: Or Charlotte Brooks and Other Slaves* [New York: Hunt and Eaton, 1890] reprint, The Schomburg Library of Nineteenth-Century Black Women Writers, ed. by Henry Louis Gates, Jr. (New York: Oxford University Press, 1988). pp. 55–56.

21. Buti Tlhagale, "Towards a Black Theology of Labor," in *The Three-Fold Cord: Theology, Work and Labour,* ed. James R. Cochrane and Gerald 0. West (Hilton, Republic of South Africa: Cluster Publications, 1991), p. 147.

Bibliography

The African Observer: A Monthly Journal. Philadelphia, 1828.

Albert, Octavia V. Rogers. *The House of Bondage: Or Charlotte Brooks and Other Slaves.* New York: Hunt and Eaton, 1890. Reprinted, The Schomburg Library of Nineteenth-Century Black Women Writers, edited by Henry Louis Gates, Jr. New York: Oxford University Press, 1988.

Alexander, Adele Logan. *Ambiguous Lives: Free Women of Color in Rural Georgia, 1789–1879.* Fayetteville, Ark: The University of Arkansas Press, 1991.

Althaus, Paul. *The Ethics of Martin Luther.* Philadelphia: Fortress Press, 1972.

Alves, Abel Athoughuia. "The Christian Social Organism and Social Welfare: The Case of Vives, Calvin, and Loyola." *Sixteenth Century Journal,* vol. XX, no. 1 (1989).

Andolsen, Barbara Hilkert. *Good Work at the Video Display Terminal—A Feminist Ethical Analysis of Clerical Work.* Knoxville, Tenn.: University of Tennessee Press, 1989.

Andrews, William L. *To Tell a Free Story: The First Century of Afro-American Autobiography, 1760–1865.* Urbana, Ill.: University of Illinois Press, 1988.

Arendt, Hannah. *The Human Condition.* Chicago: University of Chicago Press, 1958.

Asante, Molefi Kete. *The Afrocentric Idea.* Philadelphia: Temple University Press, 1987.

Asante, Molefi Kete, and Kariamu Welsh Asante, eds. *African Culture: The Rhythms of Unity.* Westport, Conn.: Greenwood Press, 1985.

Aunt Sally or the Cross the Way of Freedom: A Narrative of the Slave-Life and Purchase of the Mother of Rev. Isaac Williams of Detroit, Michigan. Cincinnati: American Reform Tract and Book Society, 1858. Reprinted, Miami: Mnemosyne Publishing Co., 1969.

Barrett, Leonard E. *Soul-Force: African Heritage in Afro-American Religion.* Garden City, N.J: Anchor Press/ Doubleday & Co., 1974.

Bastide, Roger. *African Civilizations in the New World.* Translated by Peter Green. London: C. Hurst & Co., 1966.

———. *The African Religions of Brazil: Toward a Sociology of the Interpenetration of Civilizations.* Baltimore: Johns Hopkins University Press, 1987.

Baxter, Richard. *The Practical Works of Richard Baxter in Four Volumes.* Ligonier, Penn.: Soil Deo Gloria Publications, 1990.

Benberry, Cuesta. *Always There: The African American Presence in American Quilts.* Louisville, Ky.: The Kentucky Quilt Project, Inc., 1992.

Bennett, Lerone, Jr. *The Shaping of Black America: The Struggles and Triumphs of African Americans, 1619 to the 1990's.* New York: Penguin Books, 1993.

Berlin, Ira, and Philip D. Morgan, eds. *Cultivation and Culture: Labor and the Shaping of Slave Life in the Americas.* Charlottesville, Va.: University Press of Virginia, 1993.

Berlin, Ira, et al. *Slaves No More: Three Essays on Emancipation and the Civil War.* New York: Cambridge, University Press, 1992.

Bertelson, David. *The Lazy South.* New York: Oxford University Press, 1967.

Blassingame, John W., ed. *Slave Testimony: Two Centuries of Letters, Speeches, Interviews, and Autobiographies.* Baton Rouge, La.: Louisiana State University Press, 1977.

————. *The Slave Community: Plantation Life in the Antebellum South.* New York: Oxford University Press, 1979.

Botkin, B. A., ed. *Lay My Burden Down: A Folk History of Slavery.* New York: A Delta Book, Dell Publishing Group, 1994.

Bourdieu, Pierre. *Outline of a Theory of Practice.* Translated by Richard Nice. Cambridge: Cambridge University Press, 1977. Reprinted, 1991.

————. *Distinction: A Social Critique of the Judgement of Taste.* London: Routledge & Kegan Paul, 1984.

————. *The Logic of Practice.* Stanford, Ca.: Stanford University Press, 1990.

————. *In Other Words: Essays Toward a Reflexive Sociology.* Cambridge, Mass.: Polity Press, 1990.

————. *Language and Symbolic Power.* Translated by Gino Raymond and Matthew Adamson. Cambridge, Mass.: Harvard University Press, 1991.

————. "The Three Forms of Theoretical Knowledge." *Social Science Information,* vol. 12 (February-June 1973): 53–80.

————. "Men and Machines." In *Advances in Social Theory & Methodology: Toward An Integration of Micro—and Macro Sociologies,* edited by Karen Knorr-Cetina and A. V. Cicourel, 304–17. Boston: Routlege & Paul Kegan, 1981.

————. "The Social Space and the Genesis of Groups." *Theory and Society: Renewal and Critique in Social Theory,* vol. 14, no. 6 (November 1985): 723–743.

————. "The Forms of Capital." In *Handbook of Theory & Research for the Sociology of Education,* edited by John G. Richardson, 241–258. Westport, Conn.: Greenwood Press, 1986.

————. "Social Space and Symbolic Power." *Sociological Theory,* vol. 7, no. 1 (spring 1989): 14–25.

————. "Legitimation and Structured Interests in Weber's Sociology of Religion." In *Max Weber, Rationality and Modernity.* Edited by Sam Whimster and Scott Lash. London: Allen and Unwin, Ltd., 1987.

Bourdieu, Pierre and Loic J. D. Wacquant. *An Invitation to Reflexive Sociology.* Chicago: University of Chicago Press, 1992.

Bouwsma, William J. *John Calvin: A Sixteenth Century Portrait.* New York: Oxford University Press, 1988.

Brandon, George. "Sacrificial Practices in Santeria, an African-Cuban Religion in the United States." In *Africanisms in American Culture,* edited by Joseph E. Holloway, 119–147. Bloomington, Ind.: Indiana University Press, 1990.

Braxton, Joanne M. *Black Women Writing Autobiography: A Tradition within a Tradition.* Philadelphia: Temple University Press, 1989.

Brown, Karen McCarthy, "Systematic Remembering, Systematic Forgetting: Ogou in Haiti." In *Africa's Ogun: Old World and New,* edited by Sandra T. Barnes, 65–89. Bloomington, Ind.: Indiana University Press, 1989.

————. "Moma Lola and the Ezilis: Themes of Mothering and Loving in Haitian Vodou." In *Unspoken Worlds: Women's Religious Lives,* edited by Nancy Auer Falk and Rita M. Gross, 235–45. Belmont, Ca.: Wadsworth Publishing Co., 1989.

Brubaker, Rogers. "Rethinking Classical Theory: The Sociological Vision of Pierre Bourdieu." *Theory and Society: Renewal and Critique in Social Theory,* vol. 14, no. 6 (November 1985): 745–75.

Bush, Barbara. *Slave Women in Caribbean Society 1650–1838.* Bloomington, Ind.: Indiana University Press, 1990.

Calvin, John. *Institutes of the Christian Religion,* vol. 1, edited by John T. McNeill. *The Library of Christian Classics,* vol. XX. Philadelphia: Westminster Press, 1955.

————. *Instruction in Faith (1537).* Translated and edited by Paul T. Fuhrmann. Louisville, Ky.: Westminster/John Knox Press, 1977.

Cannon, Katie G. *Black Womanist Ethics,* American Academy of Religion Series, no. 60. Atlanta: Scholars Press, 1988.

————. *Katie's Canon.* New York: Continuum Publishing Co., 1995.

————. "Slave Ideology and Biblical Interpretation." *Semeia,* vol. 47, (1989): 9–23.

————. "The Emergence of Black Feminist Consciousness." In *Feminist Interpretation of the Bible,* edited by Letty M. Russell. Philadelphia: Westminster Press, 1985.

————. "Surviving the Blight." In *Inheriting Our Mothers' Gardens: Feminist Theology in Third World Perspective,* edited by Letty M. Russell, et al. Philadelphia: Westminster Press, 1988.

Carby, Hazel V. *Reconstructing Womanhood: The Emergence of the Afro-American Woman Novelist.* New York: Oxford University Press, 1987.

Chang, Patricia Mei Yin. "Beyond the Clan: A Re-analysis of the Empirical Evidence in Durkheim's *The Elementary Forms of the Religious Life*." *Sociological Theory,* vol. 7, no.1 (spring 1989): 64–69.

Childress, James F., and John Macquarrie, eds. *The Dictionary of Christian Ethics.* Philadelphia: Westminster, 1986.

Clinton, Catherine. *The Plantation Mistress: Woman's World in the Old South.* New York: Pantheon Books. 1982.

The Colored American. New York City, 1837–1841.

Comaroff, Jean. *Body of Power, Spirit of Resistance: The Culture and History of a South African People.* Chicago: University of Chicago Press, 1985.

Cone, James. *God of the Oppressed.* San Francisco: Harper & Row, 1975.

Copeland, M. Shawn. "Wading through Many Sorrows: Toward a Theology of Suffering in Womanist Perspective." In *A Troubling in My Soul: Womanist Perspectives on Evil and Suffering,* edited by Emilie M. Townes. Maryknoll, N.Y: Orbis Books, 1993.

Copher, Charles B. "3,000 Years of Biblical Interpretation with Reference to Black Peoples." *Journal of the Interdenominational Theological Center,* vol. 30, no. 2 (spring 1986): 225–46.

Courlander, Harold. *Negro Folk Music, U.S.A.* New York: Columbia University Press, 1963.

Croatto, J. Severino. *Biblical Hermeneutics: Toward a Theory of Reading as the Production of Meaning.* Maryknoll, N.Y.: Orbis Books, 1987.

Davis, Angela. *The Angela Davis Reader.* Edited by Joy James. Malden, Mass.: Blackwell Publishers, 1998.

———. "Reflections on the Black Woman's Role in the Community of Slaves." *The Black Scholar,* vol. 3 (December 1971): 3–15.

Davis, Charles T., and Henry Louis Gates, Jr. *The Slave's Narrative.* New York: Oxford University Press, 1985.

Davis, David Brion. "Slavery and the Meaning of America." 1966. Reprint. *Myth and Southern History, Vol. 1: The Old South,* 2nd. ed. Edited by Patrick Gerster and Nicholas Cords, 31–40. Urbana, Ill.: University of Illinois Press, 1989.

Delaney, Lucy A. *From the Darkness Cometh the Light, or Struggles for Freedom.* St. Louis: J. T. Smith Publishing House, c. 1891. Reprinted, The Schomburg Library of Nineteenth-Century Black Women Writers, *Six Women's Slave Narratives,* edited by Henry Louis Gates, Jr. New York: Oxford University Press, 1988.

Douglass' Monthly, Rochester, N.Y. vol. 1, no. 8, January 1859, pp. 12–13, in *Negro Periodicals in the United States: The Black Experience in America.* New York: Negro University Press, 1969.

Douglass, Frederick. *My Bondage and My Freedom.* 1855. Reprinted. New York: Dover Publications, Inc., 1969.

Douglass, Jane Dempsey. *Women, Freedom, and Calvin.* Philadelphia: Westminster Press, 1985.

Earl, Riggins R., Jr. *Dark Symbols, Obscure Signs: God, Self, and Community in the Slave Mind.* Maryknoll, N.Y.: Orbis Books, 1993.

Elizabeth. *The Memoir of Old Elizabeth, A Coloured Woman.* Philadelphia: Collins Printer, 1863. Reprint. The Schomburg Library of Nineteenth-Century Black Women Writers, *Six Women's Slave Narratives,* edited by Henry Louis Gates, Jr. New York: Oxford University Press, 1988.

Elkins, Stanley. *Slavery: A Problem in American Institutional and Intellectual Life,* 3rd edition revised. Chicago: University of Chicago Press, 1976.

Escott, Paul D. *Slavery Remembered: The Twentieth Century Slave Narratives.* Chapel Hill, N.C.: University of North Carolina Press, 1979.

————. "The Art and Science of Reading WPA Slave Narratives." In *The Slave's Narrative,* edited by Charles T. Davis and Henry Louis Gates, Jr. New York: Oxford University Press, 1985.

Exum, Cheryl. "You Shall Let Every Daughter Live: A Study of Exodus 1:8–2:10." *Semeia,* vol. 28 (1983).

————. "Second Thoughts about Secondary Characters: Women in Exodus 1:8–2:10." In *A Feminist Companion to Exodus to Deuteronomy,* edited by Athalya Brenner. Sheffield: Sheffield Academic Press, 1994.

Faust, Drew Gilpin. *James Henry Hammond and the Old South: A Design for Mastery.* Baton Rouge, La.: Louisiana State University Press, 1982.

————. *Southern Stories: Slaveholders in Peace and War.* Columbia, Mo.: University of Missouri Press, 1992.

Featherstone, Mike. "French Social Theory: An Introduction." *Theory Culture & Society,* vol 3, no. 3 (1986): 1–6.

Felder, Cain Hope, ed. *Stony the Road We Trod: African American Biblical Interpretation.* Minneapolis: Fortress Press, 1991.

————. *Troubling Biblical Waters: Race, Class, and Family.* Maryknoll, N.Y.: Orbis Books, 1990.

Fogel, Robert William. *Without Consent or Contract: The Rise and Fall of American Slavery.* New York: W. W. Norton & Co,, 1989.

Fogel, Robert William and Stanley L. Engerman. *Time on the Cross: The Economics of American Negro Slavery.* New York: W. W. Norton & Co., 1989.

Foner, Philip S., and Ronald L. Lewis, eds. *Black Workers: A Documentary History from Colonial Times to the Present.* Philadelphia: Temple University Press, 1989.

Foster, Frances Smith. *Witnessing Slavery: The Development of Ante-Bellum Slave Narratives.* Madison, Wis.: The University of Wisconsin Press, 1979.

————. *Written by Herself: Literary Production by African American Women, 1746–1892.* Bloomington, Ind.: Indiana University Press, 1993.

Fox-Genovese, Elizabeth and Eugene D. Genovese, "The Divine Sanction of Social Order: Religious Foundations of the Southern Slaveholders' World View." *Journal of the American Academy of Religion,* vol. LV, no. 2 (summer 1987): 211–233.

Fox-Genovese, Elizabeth. *Within the Plantation Household: Black and White Women of the Old South.* Chapel Hill, N.C.: The University of North Carolina Press, 1988.

Frazier, E. Franklin. *The Negro Church in America.* New York: Schocken Books, 1964.

Fredrickson, George M. *The Arrogance of Race: Historical Perspectives on Slavery, Racism, and Social Inequality.* Middletown, Conn.: Wesleyan University Press, 1988.

Freitheim, Terrence. *Exodus: Interpretation—A Bible Commentary for Teaching and Preaching.* Louisville, Ky.: John Knox Press, 1991.

Frye, Gladys-Marie. *Stitches From The Soul: Slave Quilts from the Antebellum South.* New York: E. P. Dutton, 1990.

Gaspar, David Barry and Darlene Clark Hine, eds. *More than Chattel: Black Women and Slavery in the Americas.* Bloomington, Ind.: Indiana University Press, 1996.

Geertz, Clifford. *The Interpretation of Cultures.* New York: Basic Books, 1973.

Genovese, Eugene D. *The Political Economy of Slavery: Studies in the Economy and Society of the Slave South.* Middletown, Conn.: Wesleyan University Press, 1989.

———. *Roll, Jordan, Roll—The World the Slaves Made.* New York: Vintage Books, 1976.

———. *The Slaveholders' Dilemma: Freedom and Progress in Southern Conservative Thought, 1820–1860.* Columbia, S.C.: University of South Carolina Press, 1992.

———. *The World the Slaveholders Made: Two Essays in Interpretation.* Middletown, Conn.: Wesleyan University Press, 1969.

Gilbert, James B. *Work without Salvation: America's Intellectual and Industrial Alienation, 1880–1910.* Baltimore: Johns Hopkins University Press, 1977.

Grant, Jacquelyn. *White Women's Christ and Black Women's Jesus: Feminist Christology and Womanist Response.* Atlanta: Scholars Press, 1989.

Greenberg, Mark. "Two Years After: What Do We Know about How the Personal Responsibility Act and Work Opportunity Reconciliation Act Is Affecting Families?" In *Shaping the Values That Shape Us: A National Consultation on Welfare Reform.* New York: The National Council of Churches of Christ in the U.S.A., 1998.

Grossman, Hildreth Y., and Nia Lane Chester. eds. *The Experience & Meaning of Work in Women's Lives.* Hillsdale, N.J.: Lawrence Erlbaum Associates, 1990.

Gutman, Herbert G. *The Black Family in Slavery and Freedom 1750–1925.* New York: Vintage Books, 1977.

Gutman, Herbert G. and Richard Sutch, "Sambo Makes Good, or Were Slaves Imbued with the Protestant Work Ethic." In *Reckoning with Slavery: A Critical Study in the Quantitative History of American Negro Slavery,* edited by Paul A. David, et al., 55–93. New York: Oxford University Press, 1976.

Hancock, LynNell. "Consultation on Welfare and the Media." In *Shaping the Values That Shape Us: A National Consultation on Welfare Reform,* 30–34. New York: The National Council of Churches of Christ in the U.S.A., 1998.

Harding, Vincent. *The Other American Revolution.* Los Angeles: CAAS, University of California and Atlanta, Ga.: Institute of the Black World, 1980.

Harrelson, Walter. "Life, Faith, and the Emergence of Tradition." In *Tradition and Theology in the Old Testament,* edited by Douglas A. Knight, 11–30. London: SPCK Press, 1977.

Harris, William. "Work and the Family in Black Atlanta." In *Black Women in United States History,* vol. II, edited by Darlene Clark Hine, 591–602. Brooklyn, N.Y.: Carlson Publishing Co., 1990.

Harrison, Beverly W. *Making the Connections: Essays in Feminist Social Ethics.* Edited by Carol S. Robb. Boston: Beacon Press, 1985.

Hauss, Jon. "Perilous Passages in Harriet Jacobs' Incidents in the Life of a Slave Girl." In *The Discourse of Slavery: Aphra Behn to Toni Morrison,* edited by Carl Plasa and Betty Ring, 144–65. London: Routledge & Kegan Paul, 1994.

Henry, R. M., "The Police Control of the Slave in South Carolina." (Ph.D. dissertation, Vanderbilt University, 1914.)

Herskovits, Melville J. *The Myth of the Negro Past.* Boston: Beacon Press, 1990.

Hine, Darlene Clark. "Lifting the Veil, Shattering the Silence: Black Women's History in Slavery and Freedom." In *Afro-American History: Past and Present,* edited by Darlene Clark Hine, 223–249. Baton Rouge, La.: Louisiana State University Press, 1986.

———. ed. *Black Women in United States History,* vols. 1–4. Brooklyn, N.Y.: Carlson, 1990.

———. ed. *Black Women in America: An Historical Encyclopedia.* Brooklyn, N.Y.: Carlson Publishing Co., 1993.

Honneth, Alex. "Fragmented World of Symbolic Forms: Reflections on Pierre Bourdieu's Sociology of Culture." *Theory Culture & Society,* vol. 3, no. 3 (1986): 55–66.

Honneth, Alex, Hermann Kocyba, and Bernard Schwibs. "The Struggle for Symbolic Order: An Interview with Pierre Bourdieu." *Theory Culture & Society,* vol. 3, no. 3 (1986): 35–51.

Hopkins, Dwight N. *Shoes That Fit Our Feet: Sources for a Constructive Black Theology.* Maryknoll, N.Y.: Orbis Books, 1993.

Hopkins, Dwight N., and George C. L. Cummings, eds. *Cut Loose Your Stammering Tongue: The Slave Narrative in Black Theology.* Maryknoll, N.Y.: Orbis Books, 1991.

Hudson, Larry E., ed. *Working Toward Freedom: Slave Society and Domestic Economy in the American South.* Rochester, N.Y.: University of Rochester Press, 1994.

Hurston, Zora Neale, *Mules and Men.* Bloomington, Ind.: Indiana University Press, 1935.

Innes, Stephen. *Creating the Commonwealth: The Economic Culture of Puritan New England.* New York: W. W. Norton & Co., 1995.

Jacobs, Donald M., ed. *Antebellum Black Newspapers: Indices to New York Freedom Journal (1827–1829), The Rights of All (1829), The Weekly Advocate (1837), and The Colored American (1837–1841).* Westport, Conn.: Greenwood Press, 1976.

Jacobs, Harriet A. *Incidents in the Life of a Slave Girl. Written by Herself.* Edited by L. Maria Child (1861). Edited by Jean Fagan Yellin. Cambridge, Mass.: Harvard University Press, 1987.

Jaynes, Gerald D. *Branches without Roots: Genesis of the Black Working Class in the American South 1862–1882.* New York: Oxford University Press, 1986.

———. "Plantation Factories and the Slave Work Ethic." In *The Slave's Narrative,* edited by Charles T. Davis and Henry Louis Gates, Jr., 98–112. New York: Oxford University Press, 1985.

Jenkins, Ralph. *Pierre Boudieu.* Key Sociologists Series. London: Routledge & Kegan Paul, 1992.

Jewell, K. Sue. *From Mammy to Miss America and Beyond: Cultural Images and the Shaping of U.S. Social Policy.* London: Routledge & Kegan Paul, 1993.

Johnson, Clifton H., ed. *God Struck Me Dead: Voices of Ex-Slaves.* Cleveland, Ohio: Pilgrim Press, 1969.

Jones, Jacqueline. *Labor of Love, Labor of Sorrow: Black Women, Work and the Family, from Slavery to the Present.* New York: Vintage Books, 1985.

———. *American Work: Four Centuries of Black and White Labor.* New York: W. W. Norton & Co., 1998.

Jones, Lawrence N., "Black Christians in Antebellum America: In Quest of the Beloved Community." *Journal of Black Thought,* vol. 38, no. 1 (summer 1987): 12–19.

Joppke, Christian. "The Cultural Dimensions of Class Formation and Class Struggle: On the Social Theory of Pierre Bourdieu." *Berkeley Journal of Sociology,* vol. 31 (1986): 53–78.

Jordan, Winthrop D. *White over Black: American Attitudes toward the Negro, 1550–1812,* Revised. New York: W. W. Norton & Co., 1977.

Joyner, Charles. *Down by the Riverside: A South Carolina Slave Community.* Urbana, Ill.: University of Illinois Press, 1984.

Keesecker, William F., ed. *A Calvin Reader: Reflections on Living.* Philadelphia: Westminster Press, 1985.

Kemble, Frances Anne. *Journal of a Residence on a Georgian Plantation in 1838–1839.* Athens, Ga.: Brown Thrasher Books, University of Georgia Press, 1984.

Kleckley, Elizabeth. *Behind the Scenes, or Thirty Years a Slave and Four Years in the White House.* New York: G. W. Carlton, 1868. Reprinted. The Schomburg Library of Nineteenth-Century Black Women Writers, edited by Henry Louis Gates, Jr. New York: Oxford University Press, 1988.

Knight, Douglas A., ed. *Tradition and Theology in the Old Testament.* London: SPCK, 1977.

Larison, C. W. *Silvia DuBois, A Biografy of A Slav Who Whipt Her Mistress and Gand Her Freedom.* The Schomburg Library of Nineteenth-Century Black Women Writers, edited by Henry Louis Gates, Jr. New York: Oxford University Press, 1988.

Lee, Orville, III. "Observations on Anthropological Thinking about the Culture Concept: Clifford Geertz and Pierre Bourdieu." *Berkeley Journal of Sociology,* vol. 33 (1988): 115–30.

Lerner, Gerda, ed. *Black Women in White America: A Documentary History.* New York: Vintage Books, 1973.

Levine, Lawrence. *Black Culture and Black Consciousness: Afro-American Folk Thought from Slavery to Freedom.* Oxford: Oxford University Press, 1977.

Lincoln, C. Eric, ed. *The Black Experience in Religion.* Garden City, N.J.: Anchor Press/Doubleday, 1974.

Litwack, Leon F. *Been in the Storm So Long: The Aftermath of Slavery.* New York: Alfred A. Knopf, 1979.

Luther, Martin. *Luther's Works,* vol. 44. Edited by Helmut Lehmann. Philadelphia: Fortress Press, 1966.

Malveaux, Julianne. "Section Introduction to Employment Issues." In *Slipping through the Cracks: The Status of Black Women,* edited by Margaret Simms and Julianne Malveaux. New Brunswick, N.J.: Transaction Publishers, 1986.

Marquardt, Manfred. *John Wesley's Social Ethics: Praxis and Principles.* Nashville: Abingdon Press, 1992.

Martin, Clarice J. "A Chamberlain's Journey and the Challenge of Interpretation for Liberation," *Semeia* 47 (1989): 105–35.

Mathews, Donald G. *Religion in the Old South.* Chicago: University of Chicago Press, 1977.

———. *Slavery and Methodism: A Chapter in American Morality, 1780–1845.* Princeton, N.J.: Princeton University Press, 1965.

Mattison, Hiram. *Louisa Picquet, the Octoroon: or A Tale of Southern Slave Life.* 1861. The Schomburg Library of Nineteenth-Century Black Women Writers, *Collected Black Women's Narratives.* Edited by Henry Louis Gates, Jr. New York: Oxford University Press, 1988.

Mbiti, John S. *African Religions and Philosophy.* Garden City, N.Y.: Doubleday & Co., 1969.

McCloud, Aminah Beverly. "A Response to *Modern Work and Human Meaning.*" Unpublished manuscript, 1986.

McGary, Howard and Bill E. Lawson. *Between Slavery and Freedom: Philosophy and American Slavery.* Bloomington, Ind.: University of Indiana Press, 1992.

McNeill, John T. *The History and Character of Calvinism.* New York: Oxford University Press, 1967.

Mellon, James, ed. *Bullwhip Days: The Slaves Remember: An Oral History.* New York: Avon Books, 1988.

Meier, August, and Elliot Rudwick. *Black History and the Historical Profession, 1915–1980.* Chicago: University of Illinois Press, 1986.

Mintz, Sydney, and Richard Price. *The Birth of African American Culture: An Anthropological Perspective.* Boston: Beacon Press, 1992.

Moi, Toril. "Appropriating Bourdieu: Feminist Theory and Pierre Bourdieu's Sociology of Culture," *New Literary History: A Journal of Theory and Interpretation,* vol. 22, no. 4 (autumn 1991): 1,017–1,049.

Moltmann, Jürgen. *On Human Dignity: Political Theology and Ethics.* Philadelphia: Fortress Press, 1984.

Monter, E. William. *Calvin's Geneva.* New York: John Wiley & Sons, 1967.

Moore, William E. *American Negro Slavery and Abolition.* New York: Third World Press, 1971.

Morgan, Edmund S. "The Puritan Ethic and the American Revolution." *The William and Mary Quarterly,* vol. 24, no. 1 (January 1967): 3–43.

Morrissey, Marietta. *Slave Women in the New World: Gender Stratification in the Caribbean.* Lawrence, Kans.: University of Kansas, 1989.

Neverdon-Morton, Cynthia. *Afro-American Women of the South and the Advancement of the Race, 1895–1925.* Knoxville, Tenn.: The University of Tennessee Press, 1989.

Newman, Katherine S. *No Shame in My Game: The Working Poor in the Inner City.* New York: Alfred A. Knopf and The Russell Sage Foundation, 1999.

Niesel, Wilhelm. *The Theology of Calvin.* Trans. Harold Knight. Philadelphia: Westminster Press, 1956.

Paris, Peter J. *The Social Teaching of the Black Churches.* Philadelphia: Fortress Press, 1985.

———. *The Spirituality of African Peoples: The Search for a Common Moral Discourse.* Minneapolis: Fortress Press, 1995.

Parish, Peter J. *Slavery: History and Historians.* New York: Harper & Row, 1989.

Perdue, Charles L., Jr., Thomas E. Barden, and Robert K. Phillips, eds. *Weevils in the Wheat: Interviews with Virginia Ex-Slaves.* Bloomington, Ind.: Indiana University Press, 1980.

Phillips, John Edward. "The African Heritage in White America." In *Africanisms in American Culture,* edited by Joseph E. Holloway, 225–39. Bloomington, Ind.: Indiana University Press, 1990.

Pine, Nicola. "Labor Exploitation in U.S. Prisons: A New Slave Labor." In *Women Against Military Madness Newsletter,* vol. 15, no. 4, May 1997.

Plasa, Carl, and Betty Ring, eds. *The Discourse of Slavery: Aphra Behn to Toni Morrison.* London: Routledge & Kegan Paul, 1994.

Preston, Ronald. *The Future of Christian Ethics.* London: SCM Press, 1987.

Quarles, Benjamin. *Black Abolitionists.* New York: Oxford University Press, 1969.

————. *Black Mosaic: Essays in Afro-American History and Historiography.* Amherst, Mass.: University of Massachusetts Press, 1988.

Raboteau, Albert J. *Slave Religion: The Invisible Institution in the Antebellum South.* New York: Oxford University Press, 1978.

Rawick, George P. "Some Notes on a Social Analysis of Slavery: A Critical Assessment of *The Slave Community.*" In *Revisiting Blassingame's The Slave Community: The Scholars Respond,* edited by Al-Tony Gilmore, 17–26. Westport, Conn.: Greenwood Publishing Co., 1978.

————. ed. *The American Slave: A Composite Autobiography.* 41 Vols. Westport, Conn.: Greenwood Publishing Co., 1972.

————, ed. *From Sundown to Sunup: The Making of the Black Community.* Vol. 1, *The American Slave.* Westport, Conn.: Greenwood Publishing Co., 1972.

Richardson, Alan. *The Biblical Doctrine of Work.* Ecumenical Biblical Studies No. 1. London: SCM Press, 1952.

Rifkin, Jeremy. *The End of Work: The Decline of the Global Labor Force and the Dawn of the Post-Market Era.* New York: G. P. Putnam's Sons, 1995.

Riggs, Marcia Y. *Awake Arise & Act: A Womanist Call for Black Liberation.* Cleveland, Ohio: Pilgrim Press, 1994.

The Rights of All. (New York City) (1829).

Ripley, C. Peter, ed. *The Black Abolitionist Papers.* 5 Vols. Chapel Hill, N.C.: University of North Carolina Press, 1985.

Rodgers, Daniel T. *The Work Ethic in Industrial America: 1850–1920.* Chicago: University of Chicago Press, 1978.

Sanders, Cheryl J. "Roundtable Discussion: Christian Ethics and Theology in Womanist Perspective: A Final Rejoinder." In *Journal of Feminist Studies in Religion,* vol. 5, no. 2 (1989): 83–91.

Scott, James C. *Domination and the Arts of Resistance: Hidden Transcripts.* New Haven, Conn.: Yale University Press, 1990.

————. *The Moral Economy of the Peasant: Rebellion and Subsistence in Southeast Asia.* New Haven, Conn.: Yale University Press, 1976.

Sobel, Mechal. *The World They Made Together: Black and White Values in Eighteenth-Century Virginia.* Princeton, N.J.: Princeton University Press, 1987.

————. *Trabelin' On: The Slave Journey to an Afro-Baptist Faith.* Princeton, N.J.: Princeton University Press, 1979.

Söelle, Dorothee with Shirley Cloyes. *To Work and to Love: A Theology of Creation.* Philadelphia: Fortress Press, 1984.

The Southern Workman. Hampton, Virginia, 1872–1879.

Stamp, Kenneth M. *The Peculiar Institution: Slavery in the Ante-Bellum South.* New York: Vintage Books, 1956.

Starling, Marion. *The Slave Narrative: Its Place in American History.* 2nd. ed. Washington, D.C.: Howard University Press, 1988.

Sterling, Dorothy, ed. *We Are Your Sisters: Black Women in the Nineteenth Century.* New York: W. W. Norton & Co., 1984.

Stuckey, Sterling. *Slave Culture: Nationalist Theory and the Foundations of Black America.* New York: Oxford University Press, 1987.

————. "Through the Prism of Folklore." *The Massachusetts Review,* vol. 9 (1968): 417–37.

Tawney, R. H. *Religion and The Rise of Capitalism.* New York: Harcourt, Brace & Co., 1926.

Tlhagale, Buti. "Towards a Black Theology of Labor." In *The Three-Fold Cord: Theology, Work and Labour,* edited by James R. Cochrane and Gerald O. West. Hilton, Republic of South Africa: Cluster Publications, 1991.

Townes, Emilie M. *In a Blaze of Glory: Womanist Spirituality as Social Witness.* Nashville: Abingdon Press, 1995.

————. *Womanist Justice, Womanist Hope, Womanist Justice.* Atlanta: Scholars Press, 1993.

————. ed. *A Troubling in My Soul: Womanist Perspectives on Evil and Suffering.* Maryknoll, N.Y.: Orbis Books, 1993.

Trible, Phyllis. "Depatriachalizing in Biblical Interpretation." *Journal of the American Academy of Religion,* vol. 41 (1973).

Troeltsch, Ernst. *The Social Teachings of the Christian Churches.* Vol. 2. Chicago: University of Chicago Press, 1981.

U. S. Department of Labor, Bureau of Labor Statistics. *History of the Federal Minimum Wage Rates Under Fair Labor Standards Act, 1938–1996.* August 1999 [cited November 6, 1999]. Available from http://www.dol.gov/dol/esa/public/ minwage/chart.htm.

————. *Report on Futurework: Trends and Challenges for Work in the 21st Century.* August 1999 [cited November 15, 1999]. Available from http://www.dol/asp/public/future/report/ chapter1/main2.htm#5b.

Veney, Bethany. *The Narrative of Bethany Veney—A Slave Woman.* Worcester, Mass.: George Ellis, Publisher, 1889. Reprinted in *Col-*

lected Black Women's Narratives, The Schomburg Library of Nineteenth-Century Black Women Writers, ed. Henry Louis Gates, Jr. New York: Oxford University Press, 1988.

Wacquant, Loric J. D. "Toward a Reflexive Sociology: A Workshop with Pierre Bourdieu." *Sociological Theory,* vol. 7, no.1 (spring 1989): 26–63.

Walker, Clarence E. *Deromanticizing Black History: Critical Essays and Reappraisals.* Knoxville, Tenn.: University of Tennessee Press, 1991.

Washington, Margaret, ed. *Narrative of Sojourner Truth.* New York: Vintage Classics, 1993.

Washington, Booker T. *Up from Slavery.* New York: Penguin Classics, 1986.

Walker, Alice. *In Search of Our Mothers' Gardens: Womanist Prose.* New York: Harcourt Brace Jovanovich, 1983.

Webber, Thomas L. *Deep Like Rivers: Education in the Slave Quarter Community, 1831–1865.* New York: W. W. Norton & Co., 1978.

Weber, Max. *The Protestant Ethic and the Spirit of Capitalism.* New York: Charles Scribner's Sons, 1958.

The Weekly Advocate. New York City, 1837.

Weems, Renita. "Reading Her Way through the Struggle: African American Women and the Bible." In *Stony the Road We Trod: African American Biblical Interpretation,* edited by Cain Felder. Minneapolis: Fortress Press, 1991.

West, Traci C. "Generating a Christian Ethical Approach to 'Welfare Reform.'" In *Shaping the Values That Shape Us: A National Consultation on Welfare Reform.* New York: The National Council of Churches of Christ in the U.S.A., 1998.

White, Deborah Gray. *Ar'nt I a Woman: Female Slaves in the Plantation South.* New York: W. W. Norton & Co., 1985.

Williams, Delores S. *Sisters in the Wilderness: The Challenge of Womanist God-Talk.* Maryknoll, N.Y.: Orbis Books, 1993.

———. "Afrocentrism and Male-Female Relations in Church and Society." In *Living the Intersection—Womanism and Afrocentrism in Theology,* edited by Cheryl J. Sanders, Minneapolis: Fortress Press, 1995.

———. "Black Women's Surrogacy Experience and the Christian Notion of Redemption." In *After Patriarchy: Feminist Transformations of the World Religions,* edited by Paula M. Cooey, William R. Eakin, and Jay B. McDaniel. Maryknoll, N.Y.: Orbis Books, 1991.

———. "The Color of Feminism, or Speaking the Black Woman's Tongue." In *Feminist Theological Ethics—A Reader,* edited by Lois K. Daly. Louisville, Ky: Westminster/John Knox Press, 1994.

Wilmore, Gayraud S. *Black Religion and Black Radicalism: An Interpretation of the Religious History of Afro-American People.* Maryknoll, N.Y.: Orbis Books, 1989.

Wilmore, Gayraud S., and James H. Cone, eds. *Black Theology: A Documentary History,* Vol. 2. Maryknoll, N.Y.: Orbis Books, 1993.

Wilson, Theodore Branter. *The Black Codes of the South.* University, Ala: University of Alabama Press, 1965.

Winter, Gibson. "Society and Morality: The French Tradition." *Review of Religious Research,* vol. 5, no. 1 (fall 1963): 11–21.

Winthrop, D. Jordan. *White over Black: American Attitudes Towards the Negro, 1550–1812.* New York: W. W. Norton & Co., 1977.

Wittenberg, Gunther. "Old Testament Perspectives on Labour." In *The Three-Fold Cord: Theology, Work and Labour,* edited by James R. Cochrane and Gerald O. West, 92–107. Hilton, Republic of South Africa: Cluster Publications, 1991.

Wood, Betty. *Women's Work, Men's Work: The Informal Slave Economies of Lowcountry Georgia.* Athens, Ga.: University of Georgia Press, 1995.

Woodward, C. Vann. "History from Slave Sources." In *The Slave's Narrative,* edited by Charles T. Davis and Henry Louis Gates, Jr. New York: Oxford University Press, 1985.

————. "The Southern Ethic in a Puritan World." In *Myth and Southern History,* Vol. 1, 2nd ed., edited by Patrick Gerster and Nicholas Cords. Urbana, Ill.: University of Illinois Press, 1989.

Wuthnow, Robert. *Poor Richard's Principle: Recovering the American Dream through the Moral Dimension of Work, Business, and Money.* Princeton, N.J.: Princeton University Press, 1996.

Yee, Shirley J. *Black Women Abolitionists: A Study in Activism, 1828–1860.* Knoxville, Tenn.: University of Tennessee Press, 1992.

Yetman, Norman R. "The Background of the Slave Narrative Collection." *American Quarterly* 19 (1967): 534–553.

————. ed. *Voices from Slavery: The Life of American Slaves—In the Words of 100 Men and Women Who Lived It and Many Years Later Talked about It.* New York: Holt, Rinehart & Winston, 1970.

Index

Abbot, James Monroe, 102–3
African common orientations, notion of, 41–48, 159 n.23
  philosophical, 47
  religious, 47
American Freedman's Inquiry Commission (AFIC), 13
annunciation, 53–54
Asante, Molefi Kete, 45, 159 n.22

Bastide, Roger, 45–46
Baxter, Richard, 129
Bertelson, David, 36, 158 n.5
black religion, 25–26
boundary crossing, 143
Bourdieu, Pierre, 42, 55–56, 58–60, 62, 64–70, 72–73, 75, 78, 80, 160 nn.42–44, 161 nn.45, 47–48, 50, 56, 61–62; 162 nn.63–64, 66–67
Braxton, Joanne, 91
Bremer, Fredrika, 21
Brooks, Charlotte, 151
Brown, Fred, 44
Brown, Karen McCarthy, 45–46, 159 nn.17, 24
Butler, Ellen, 25, 46–47

calling, 3–4, 101, 114, 123–29, 138
  See also vocation
Calvin, John, 122–29, 168 n.37
Cannon, Katie Geneva, xi, 29–32, 50–54, 157 nn.35, 37, 38, 40–42; 160 nn.35, 37–40; 165 nn.51, 54; 169 nn.52–53
Carby, Hazel, 94, 153 n.2, 161 n.53, 165 nn.38–39
chattel slavery, 1–2, 4, 12, 23, 35–37, 39–40, 56–57, 67, 140

Christianity, 22–26
Clinton, Catherine, 95, 161 n.53, 165 n.42
Coleman, Will, 46, 159 n.26
community (communion), 152
community of resistance, 26
Cone, James, 27, 156 n.29, 157 n.33, 166 n.5
Cooper, Anna Julia, 2
Copeland, Shawn, 107, 157 n.35, 166 n.71
cult of true womanhood, 93–94

Davenport, Carey, 25
Davis, Angela, 102, 148–49, 155 n.16, 164 n.30, 170 nn.17–18
Davis, David Brion, 37–38, 158 n.8
Delaney, Lucy, 14, 100, 122, 135, 154–55 n.8, 165 n.57
  Crockett, Polly 100
dispositions, 3–4, 59–62, 65
distinction, 3–4, 42, 58
Drumgoold, Kate, 13–14, 154 nn.6–7
Du Bois, W. E. B., 15

Earl, Riggins, 27, 63, 157 n.29, 31; 161 n.58, 163 n.8
Elkins, Stanley, 35–36, 158 nn.3–4
emancipatory historiography, 50, 53–54
embodiment, 146–47
evil, 33, 105–7, 144, 146
Exum, Cheryl, 118, 167 nn.13–16

Faust, Drew, 58, 67, 161 n.46; 162 nn.68–69

187